Simply Joy

RAIN OR SHINE

*Learning to live with joy during
the sunshine and the storms*

Copyright 2021 by Jennifer Jackson

Edited by Ali Hooper; www.alihooper.com
Cover and interior design by Kreativity Inc.; www.kreativityinc.com

Table of Contents

Foreword

When I first met Jennifer, it was over lunch at a farmhouse-style restaurant. She was more familiar with the menu than I was, and I took her recommendation to order one of her favorite salads. Then she added, "Order extra croutons." With her instruction to go heavy on the carbs, I knew that we were going to get along just fine.

Within a month of our first meeting, we successfully wrote and edited a manuscript that resulted in her first published book, *A Christmas Heart*. We were a couple of energizer bunnies, plowing through the writing with long days in front of our computers, carbs and coffee. Just as quickly as we completed that project, Jennifer began making suggestions for a second book. Although we did not finish it quite as swiftly, we still cranked out a second book within only a couple of months.

More significant than the speed at which Jennifer was writing was the health journey that was unfolding in her life. During the writing of her second book, *An Easter Heart*, Jennifer received a callback from her doctor after a regularly scheduled mammogram. Confident that it was merely a just-to-be-safe follow up, Jennifer and I carried on with our meetings and writing, often over chips and salsa at a local Mexican restaurant.

But the results of those appointments were not what we hoped. Out of the blue, in the middle of the writing and pastoring and teaching, Jennifer was diagnosed with breast cancer.

Suddenly everything changed. Seemingly overnight, Jennifer was thrust into a world of tests, procedures, surgery and treatments, all happening at what felt like lightning speed. Her chemo days began to demand more and more recovery time, to the point that she was barely able to recover before the next round of intensive medication was pumped through her compromised system. Whenever she could, she returned to the book, generating content and putting words to her ideas. Our once record-breaking speed writing was now at the mercy of the cancer that she was fiercely fighting. The writing slowed. The ideas stalled. The road became hard, bumpy, treacherous and painful.

She was in a mighty battle, and all of her energy focused on her healing. As our deadlines moved back again and again and again, it often looked like God had other plans for the book. Maybe we had the wrong timing. Maybe it just wasn't meant to be. Or maybe satan was mad as you-know-what that Jennifer was writing a book on joy.

You are reading that book - the book that she wrote in between procedures, surgery, chemo treatments, trips to the bathroom, exhaustion and pain. She did it. God did it. He brought her through this season, and in addition to her healing, a book rose from the darkness of the valley.

But here is what astounds me the most about Jennifer. As she worked tirelessly through this long and hard process, she never stopped living with the joy of Jesus shining brightly from her life. Time and again, Jennifer said, "This is hard." As she persevered, she hung tightly to Jesus, and His joy spilled out. She never denied the difficult journey. She acknowledged it, and she acknowledged Jesus with her in it. As a result, she lives with an unexplainable and undeniable delight, an umbrella of warmth, hope and peace that exudes from her as she carries on.

It's no wonder that she is able to write so profoundly about the joy of the Lord. She lives it! She lives it in the good and the bad, and I know a more joy-filled Jesus because of her.

It's a privilege and gift to be part of this journey with her, and I am confident that you will encounter the joy of Jesus as you travel this joy journey too. I am especially excited because I know the power of that joy. Before long, those around you will feel it - His joy spilling from your life.

Are you ready? Are you ready for this journey of joy?

Join Jennifer on this joy journey, and discover the delight that God has for you.
And don't forget to order extra croutons.

Love and grace,
Ali Hooper

Introduction

I am deep in the heart of Kenya. The air is thick and hot. Yet, as I look around me, two obvious realities hit me in the center of my chest. One, the local residents here are strikingly beautiful, and two, their physical needs are blatantly abundant. So many people in this rural village survive without shoes on their feet, clean water to drink and adequate shelter to protect them from the never-ending heat. At our medical clinic, I visit with more than a dozen patients. Their feet show the constant dirt from fog-like dust clouds across the landscape. Without access to a convenient fresh-water source, a film of grime covers already tattered clothes loosely hanging from narrow shoulders and thin waistlines resulting from the area's pervasive food scarcity.

It is April, and I traveled twenty-four hours to Chavakali, Kenya, alongside a mission team from our church. The have-nots surround me, and also, I'm surrounded by such abundant joy. How can this be? There is clapping, dancing, singing and laughter. I look around at the faces and see eyes bright with joy, smiles full of life and hands waving in praise. How can they have so little but live as if they have so much? Why is there so much joy? Where is it coming from, and how do I get some? I want to live a life with this freedom in joy, but is it possible?

Over the years, I've had the privilege of spending many weeks in Kenya, and those visits changed me forever.

"Hear, O Lord, and be merciful to me; O Lord, be my help. You turned my wailing into dancing; you removed my sackcloth and clothed me with joy that my heart may not be silent. O Lord my God, I will give You thanks forever" (Psalm 30:10-12).

Back at home in Ohio, I am often motivated by the summer's warming temperatures to start a project that brings me a feeling of fresh hope.

I plant seeds, cover a wall with a coat of paint, redecorate a tired-looking room or squeeze and can fruit from the trees. I just love having something tangible to do as I enter into a new season.

What if this year we decided to tackle a project together? What if this year we shared in a new season together, reaching for fresh hope through a shared project - a joy project? Just as you might update your wardrobe, refinish an old dresser or sweep out the garage, let us turn the page on the calendar with a project. Let us begin a new season with a commitment to discovering everlasting joy.

Joy is a theme throughout scripture, woven into the journeys, victories, pain and sorrow of the characters and stories across its pages. This trait - joy - has been a mark of believers for many centuries. Joy isn't something you can conjure into your mind and suddenly the feeling follows, nor is it something you can fake. Trying to fake joy is unhealthy. Joy - true, everlasting joy - is sincere. It overflows from the depths of your being as an outgrowth of a genuine relationship with God.

What is Joy?

Webster defines joy as the emotion evoked by well-being, success, or good fortune or by the prospect of possessing what one desires: delight.

I created my own definition of joy: an expression of delight in the heart and mind that prevails no matter the external circumstances combined with an internal awareness of God's presence at all times.

In other words, we may not feel joy moment by moment, but it is the umbrella sheltering and protecting our lives. Every day we can choose to put on joy as we would put on sunglasses on a bright day. We can wear joy to see God more clearly despite the blinding brightness of our harsh world.

This past year a global pandemic hit the entire world, exposing vulnerabilities with a serious health and financial crisis, but a tremendous shortage that I noticed was the lack of joy. People were walking around in either panic or fog. Folks were isolated at home with their routines turned upside down, and discouragement and "the blues" were more rampant than ever. In many cases, people faced a necessary job or location change. Especially after this past year, we all need a restart, just like you would reboot your computer and get it to start up again. Joy has gone missing, and happiness is needed now more than ever.

All of us seek joy. We want to find ways to consistently feel optimistic about our lives, hopeful about our futures and warm about our feelings toward others. We look for joy in relationships, titles, exercise, money and things like a house or car. While all of these things can be good things, not one of them can sustain a life of established joy. It is only a matter of time before our eyes land on the next thing that we think will bring us joy, and we begin to live a life of "what's next?" rather than a life of sustained contentment.

In addition, when we seek joy from the touchable and the circumstantial, we set ourselves up for the experience of having our joy snatched away from us. A traffic ticket, fussy toddler, messy house or grumpy co-worker all threaten to ruin our day and steal our joy. How can we live hour-by-hour with a feeling of warmth that fulfills us and rests deep inside our soul? How can we live with the kind of joy that is so explosive that it spills out through a smile, kind word, a hearty laugh or bear hug to a hurting friend? Instead of being jealous, joy celebrates with others when they win. Joy praises the smallest accomplishments in others to encourage and support them. Joy is like a lifetime friend, always welcoming, encouraging and hope-filled. Joy laughs quickly, smiles abundantly and expresses gratitude daily. Joy is key to a godly and satisfying life.

How does joy differ from happiness?

Joy and happiness are often interchanged, but they are not the same thing.

Joy is a feeling, experience and radiating sense of delight that permeates the soul. Joy grows from within as you draw closer to God.

Joy
- looks for the good.
- encourages self and others.
- is full of laughter.
- gives freely.
- receives graciously.
- is a renewable resource.
- provides the fuel to stay steadied on God throughout the minutes, hours and days.
- enjoys Spirit-led spontaneity.
- carries you through the dark valleys of life.
- triumphs over challenges.

Joy does not cover up grief; instead, joy is a healing balm during pain. Joy doesn't ignore difficulty; rather, joy pops up in the midst of the hard, reminding us that there is good even when the circumstances tell a different story.

Happiness, on the other hand, is a feeling and experience that results from the external. While we enjoy happiness, it isn't sustainable, renewable or lasting. Happiness is tricky, sometimes temperamental and often fleeting. Happiness results from something, whereas joy is the source by which we live, pointing to hope. A solid and healthy well of joy is always accessible while happiness comes and goes like the tide. Joy is steady and transcends our circumstances, while happiness is momentary and dependent on preferential circumstances. Happiness is like a "windfall" or an added bonus, whereas joy is like a consistent, steady-paying job that brings fulfillment.

Let me be clear. There is nothing wrong with happiness! It's ok to enjoy happiness. The trouble is when we seek happiness, we soon discover that it is elusive and fleeting. The ebbs and flows of life leave us always wanting more. Joy, on the other hand, defies the odds. Joy delivers something pleasant and warm to the heart even when the world around you points toward pain, heartache, sadness or struggle. Seeking happiness is exhausting because it is temporary. However, seeking joy is life-giving because it never runs dry. Like a fresh-water spring, it promises to always satisfy. So seek joy, and discover the delight of living from a full reservoir of hope, promise and pleasure.

I've served in ministry for many years, meeting hundreds of women from all walks of life. Some have so little yet exude so much joy, while others have so much yet lack any evidence of joy. Most of us probably fall somewhere in between. When I think about joy, both living with and living without it, many women come to mind, but I want to highlight a couple of women in particular.

Sarah was a single mom, living on disability and in government housing. Her only son was in high school and on track to graduate. Despite everything she needed, despite her speech impediment, despite her lack of transportation, despite her failing health, despite it all - she lived with joy. When we prayed together, she prayed with tears streaming down her face as she pleaded for God's provision in her life.

Then, as our church family showed up as the conduit of God's provision for her and her son, she overflowed with gratitude, and her joy-filled attitude motivated the church to continue finding ways to help her. She was doing the best she could even though life had been so cruel to her. Undeniable joy filled her up! I can still picture her greeting us with a smile and a bulletin as we entered the sanctuary. I can still see her sweet hands in the air, lifted to God at church, as she sang in praise to the

Lord. When she died, I knew heaven was her home. I had no regrets for the time, money and care I had given to her family. She was pure joy, and it was a joy to love her.

Sarah is an example of someone who had nothing, yet because of Jesus, she had joy. She enjoyed her life, her church and her son. Similarly, we too can experience joy despite our situation.

I knew another woman living with everything Sarah dreamed of having, yet her attitude was completely void of joy.

Carrie and I lived near Kenwood Mall, home to my favorite store for children's clothes. The t-shirts and shorts were soft cotton colors that blended and matched adorably. On my tight budget, I only wished to buy more than a couple of outfits for my two little boys because the clothes lasted forever. So when Carrie called and said she had baskets of hand-me-down, quality boy clothes from my favorite children's clothing store, clothes that I could sort through and keep, I was beyond thrilled. She invited me to spend the day with her, visiting while we sorted clothes.

I sat on her immaculate living room floor, observing her perfectly decorated and meticulously organized home. She had a lovely centerpiece atop her dining room table. Her kitchen was stocked with every spice you could imagine and all of the latest cooking tools. She also had fashionable clothes, pretty nails, two cute dogs with matching collars and a fun, sporty car. I was impressed. Knowing that she didn't have to work because her husband had a high-paying job, I pushed down my jealousy as I was working two side jobs to help pay the bills.

Nonetheless, I enjoyed my time with her, and her generosity blew me away. However, as we visited together, I began to sense that something was missing. She seemed discontent, semi-depressed and restless as if nothing satisfied her. As we spent time together, I began to pray under my breath, "Lord, she needs You," and I wondered if I could offer a word of hope or a warm hug to make a difference in her day. I tried to share little bits about God with her, but it was as if the words bounced off the ceiling and fell flat. She was void of emotion, and she was hurting while living in a gorgeous, 3,000 square foot box that held everything this world has to offer.

Can you relate to Carrie? Or maybe you can relate to Sarah. Perhaps you have a Carrie or a Sarah in your own life. Where do you find yourself on this spectrum today? If you're like me, you can identify with both women. I've had seasons when life has been easy and breezy, yet I struggled to connect with true joy. I've also had seasons when life has been painful and complex, yet I felt immense contentment strengthening me throughout my days. I've also had many times in which the easy-breezy was joy-filled, and the painful-hard was, well, painful and hard.

My hope for you and me is that we pursue more joy no matter the circumstances surrounding us.

Are you seeking happiness or joy? What is it that you want to pursue in your life? That which is here one moment and gone the next? Or do you want to experience a firm foundation of joy that gives strength to your days, laughter in your pain and hope in the hard?

Let's discover, plant, sow and reap joy together.

I'm in this with you, and I'm cheering you on as your friend,

Jennifer

CHAPTER

1

Joy and Jesus

My earliest memories take place in a tiny ranch house in Nicholasville, Kentucky. Our home and six other houses sat on a hill surrounded by cows, trees and rolling fields. My parents grew up going to church and they knew the Lord closely, but because of a recent move and the birth of my new baby brother, we had not been attending church. That was about to change, as was my entire life.

One day my parents announced that we would attend the small community church in town. I was beyond excited. I was a super social child, and I loved meeting new people. That first Sunday at church, I eagerly entered my Sunday school classroom greeted by a kind teacher and a dozen other kids. In the middle of the room was a white, eight-foot-long folding table, and we kids sat along each side. I sat next to another little, blonde-haired girl who introduced herself to me as Rhea. We were instant friends.

That morning's lesson was about Jesus. Our teacher shared that Jesus wanted to be our friend and live inside our hearts to help us, love us and guide our lives. Drawn to this instant hope, I intently listened as she shared how God sent His only son, Jesus, to this world and He ended up on a cross to die for our sins. The teacher encouraged us to believe in this friend Jesus and invite Him to live in our hearts.

"Does anyone want to pray with me?" she said. "Does anyone want this salvation?"

I had never heard of a cross before. I didn't realize that someone would have to cover my sins. My young heart was racing as I began to think about lying to my mom, jumping on my bed and sneaking cookie dough while hiding in the closet. My many bad choices swirled around in my mind. Fresh in my thoughts was a recent time when my mom had not allowed me to attend a pool party with the neighbor girl all because of my poor choices. I knew without a doubt that I had sinned. Could God take care of all my sins? At that moment, with my heart pounding, time stood still, and I thought, "I need to make a decision." Coming back to the teacher, I looked up and said, "Yes, please, me first."

The kind teacher smiled as she turned to the other kids, "Does anyone else want to pray with us?"

Wiggling in our seats, sweet Rhea raised her hand. She also wanted this friend named Jesus. With our blonde little pigtails falling to our shoulders, we bowed our heads, folded our hands and prayed the sinner's prayer out loud. It was just me, Rhea, ten other kids and a kind teacher sitting around a white, plastic table on that memorable day.

Looking back, I'm amazed and encouraged that I had parents who taught me right from wrong, took me to church and cultivated a sense of holy living inside me even as a young child. These values build strong foundations in the Lord. If you are doing that for your family, keep going. It is worth it.

"'Surely God is my salvation; I will trust and not be afraid. The Lord, the Lord himself, is my strength and my defense; he has become my salvation.' With joy, you will draw water from the wells of salvation" (Isaiah 12:2-3).

Jesus, the Source of Joy

Falling in love with Jesus is the beginning of joy in this life. Our relationship with Jesus is so much more than a ritual or checklist. It is personal. He invites us to be transformed by His love and power day by day. I cannot think of anything else in life that guarantees such dramatic results, can you? When we connect with Jesus and allow Him to permeate our lives with His joy, He creates in us someone optimistic, at ease and enthusiastic. Isn't that compelling?

> BECAUSE JESUS IS JOY, A RELATIONSHIP WITH JESUS CONNECTS US TO AN ENDLESS SOURCE OF JOY.

Joy is the undercurrent that overflows in our hearts as His love is poured out for us. Falling in love with Jesus began for me at age seven, around that white, plastic table, in that ranch house on a hill and among my friends like Rhea. That started the unexpected process of joy in my life. Little did I realize that a relationship with God, our Creator and His only Son Jesus, would be a foundational relationship in my life. Because of this tight bond, I would surprisingly grow in the fruit of joy year after year.

My life was forever changed when I prayed at the small church in town. That was the best day of my life. Almost like a date stamped in a concrete sidewalk with my name on it, a new birthday, May 6, 1979, is when I became new - a new creation. I was a child and came as a child that incredible spring day and, yes, joy was found. I still remember the hope in knowing that Jesus would come into my heart to cover all my shameful feelings and be my forever friend. What good news! Because I so desperately wanted to be saved, I felt great wonder and comfort as a result of my salvation. For a kid, salvation was like a big bag of candy or a new toy doll. It was truly exciting to me, and I still remember that first feeling of joy when I was saved.

"...yet I will rejoice in the Lord! I will be joyful in the God of my salvation!" (Habakkuk 3:18).

A close-knit relationship with Jesus truly is the basis for developing joy in your life. So how does knowing Jesus make a difference on your joy journey?

HOW DOES KNOWING JESUS MAKE A DIFFERENCE ON YOUR JOY JOURNEY?

Joy from Scripture

Scripture is full of examples of joy found through a connection with Jesus, who is the source of joy through salvation. Here are just a few:

- In Psalm 51:11-12 David prays, "Do not cast me from your presence or take your Holy Spirit from me. Restore to me the joy of your salvation and grant me a willing spirit, to sustain me." David knows that the source of his joy is his connection with God through the Holy Spirit. Though David predated Jesus, David lived by forward-looking faith, and that faith was his joy.

- The prophet Isaiah foretold of the coming Messiah Jesus, and Isaiah wrote a song of praise linking joy with his salvation. "With joy, you will draw water from the wells of salvation" (Isaiah 12:3).

- In Acts 2 we read about Pentecost when the Holy Spirit appeared to those who had been saved by faith in Jesus. Peter said, "Save yourselves from this corrupt generation" (v40). Luke tells us that 3,000 were saved that day, and he goes on to write, "They broke bread in their homes and ate together with glad and sincere hearts, praising God and enjoying the favor of all the people" (v46-47). What a clear picture of living a life of joy as a result of salvation.

- Peter also expanded on this link between joy and saving faith when he wrote, "Though you have not seen him, you love him; and even though you do not see him now, you believe in him and are filled with an inexpressible and glorious joy" (1 Peter 1:8).

Joy from the Creator in Creation

I learned early in life to find joy in my salvation and also in Jesus as creator. In our one-acre yard, my mother filled at least half an acre with garden cucumbers, tomatoes, corn and my favorite, watermelons. My love of flowers began at the end of the garden, where my mother planted a patch of zinnias that I was allowed to pick freely. Fluffy clouds in the shapes of bears, lions and Mickey Mouse floated over the Kentucky blue sky. It was there on that hill that I learned to love God's presence in nature. I could almost see Him in the face of my white, fluffy poodle named Cotton and feel God's warmth when I wrapped my arms around my dog's neck. I tasted His goodness in every juicy, warm strawberry eaten straight from the patch. I sat on the deck of our treehouse as I intently watched cows move across the landscape and red cardinals and yellow finches fly overhead. I ran barefoot back and forth from the field to the house all summer long, feeling every cool grass blade under my feet, which I loved despite the occasional bee sting. It was all joy.

"The meadows are covered with flocks and the valleys are mantled with grain; they shout for joy and sing" (Psalm 65:13).

"Let the rivers clap their hands, let the mountains sing together for joy" (Psalm 98:8).

Even science supports the joy that is found in experiencing creation. According to an article published by Harvard Medical School's Harvard Health Publishing, interacting and engaging nature is linked to an improved mood. Many other studies support the same conclusion: an encounter with God's creation brings joy.

AN ENCOUNTER WITH GOD'S CREATION BRINGS JOY.

A fascinating fact about Jesus is that He was there with the Father from the beginning of time. He was there with God at creation. Nature is an immediate place of satisfaction in our lives. Simply look around; He is there. Once I invited Jesus into my heart, I began to see the visible gifts of joy that He brought me in the open air. I could see, feel, taste, and touch Him everywhere. Knowing that I was free from my yucky sin-filled feelings warmed my heart as did knowing that Jesus was my friend.

John 1 explains to us that Jesus is the Word and is one with God. He was there with the Father, when forming the earth, from the very beginning. He and God worked as a team to bring us divine beauty in Genesis. The Holy Spirit was also there from the start, hovering over the waters, working with God the Father and Jesus the Son for all design.

"In the beginning was the Word, and the Word was with God, and the Word was God. He was with God in the beginning. Through him all things were made; without him nothing was made that has been made" (John 1:1-3).

"Now the earth was formless and empty, darkness was over the surface of the deep, and the Spirit of God was hovering over the waters" (Genesis 1:2).

"Let the sea resound, and all that is in it; let the fields be jubilant, and everything in them! Let the trees of the forest sing, let them sing for joy before the Lord, for he comes to judge the earth. Give thanks to the Lord, for he is good; his love endures forever" (1 Chronicles 16:32-34).

AFTER ACCEPTING JESUS THAT DAY,
WITH THE JOY OF THE LORD IN MY
HEART, I IMMEDIATELY BEGAN TO SEE
THE WORLD DIFFERENTLY.

After church, on the day I prayed to receive salvation, my family went to Long John Silver's for lunch. As my adorable little sister and I sat in the booth, I remember thinking, "It's ok if she puts tons of vinegar on her fish today. Even that smell won't bother me because I'm full of joy." Nothing could wipe the smile off my face or take the spring out of my step.

Later that week, I grabbed my Girl Scouts "sit upon" (a folded vinyl tablecloth with a strap) and my small pink suitcase packed with paper, markers and art supplies. Finding a cozy spot on the farmland behind our home, I pressed down the tall grasses that desperately needed a good brush hog, and I laid down. The sky was pure blue with the occasional fluffy cloud floating by. As I rested, I prayed. I was entirely in love and talking to Jesus about everything. There in my hiding place, I painted and drew scenes for Him. I felt alive, I felt clean and I knew that Jesus was my friend. He was my eternal life.

Though I was only seven years old, the seed of joy was planted in my young heart. Like a ripe fruit that begins as a tiny seed planted in the ground, the joy of Jesus began to develop, mature and grow within my life.

"For the Lord your God will bless you in all your harvest and in all the work of your hands, and your joy will be complete" (Deuteronomy 16:15b).

Joy, A Fruit of the Spirit

My family has always had fruit trees. It's a "Jackson thing." Usually, my husband Doyle plants fruit trees on his birthday or Father's Day as a favorite gift. Additionally, both sets of my grandparents had all sorts of berry vines and fruit trees, including apple, cherry, peach and even a grape vineyard. Our heritage has planted and enjoyed bearing fruit across our many homes. Did I mention that we love fruit trees? There is something gratifying about picking a ripe apple from the limb of a tree, and the early-spring flowering branches are always show stoppers. As a result of once having trees loaded with pears, Doyle created his own secret family spiced-pear jam recipe. I love it on hot biscuits or warm homemade bread! We have enjoyed pear and apple trees throughout the years, and someday I hope to plant a plum tree. To enjoy the fruit, the trees must be sprayed and trimmed so that we can eventually pick, peel, freeze or devour the ripe, healthy fruit. This labor-intensive effort is worth the taste!

In the book of Galatians, Paul explains that the many fruits of the Holy Spirit must also be grown, tended and maintained, spiritually speaking. All holy fruits are desirable and necessary. We ought to seek after them to experience a cup-running-over type life. Of all the fruits of the Spirit, joy might be my most desired. When joy is alive and present in my life, many other unpleasant emotions such as discouragement, frustration and irritability tend to vanish.

"But the fruit of the Spirit is love, joy, peace, forbearance, kindness, goodness, faithfulness, gentleness and self-control. Against such things there is no law" (Galatians 5:22-23).

It's tempting to find other ways to shortcut the cultivation process of joy in our lives, but they simply do not work. Looking to people, success, distractions, busyness or material things is often how we seek satisfaction, but when we do, it is in vain. Ultimately we have to go back to Jesus. We cannot bear fruit apart from the source. We cannot accept the fruit of joy apart from Jesus.

> WE CANNOT ACCEPT THE FRUIT OF JOY APART FROM JESUS.

"I am the vine; you are the branches. If you remain in me and I in you, you will bear much fruit; apart from me you can do nothing" (John 15:5).

Joy in Salvation

In Kenya, we ministered to hundreds and hundreds of women all week long at our "Woman Weep Not" conference. Specifically, four hundred and fifty widows walked for miles across the countryside to attend, bringing their fatherless children along. In this setting, I experienced the fruit of joy in a way that I will never forget.

Temperatures in our meeting room were rising with the African sun. Meanwhile, voices were rising in joyous songs to the Lord. I felt the floor move with the rise and fall of their feet, keeping in step with the music. I could not get past the natural movement of their bodies in sync with every beat, accentuating the lyrics of praise to God.

I ADMIRED HOW THEY WORSHIP GOD WITH THEIR WHOLE BEING. THEY WERE TEACHING ME A BETTER WAY.

Jampacked, the room overflowed for our final celebration. Precious children, teens and orphans sang in the crowded aisles. Enamored by the gorgeous colors of their dresses and matching headwraps, I fell in love with the deep blues, royal purples and patterned fabrics mixed with bright yellow and warm coral. Energy, exuberance and pleasure, filled many of these women. As I see their complete participation, I wonder to myself How can it be? They are dancing in total abandonment to the Lord in the middle of their circumstances. So I decided to join them.

Outside we had a medical clinic set up to treat fingers and toes for "jiggers," a parasite embedded under the skin. Meanwhile, the kitchen crew was busy preparing a big treat with large vats of rice, beans and greens. Another group of incredibly obedient children met with our mission team to sing songs, play games and learn lessons about God. All of these activities continued for the entire week. The local mission team traveled throughout the surrounding rural areas and knocked on each door to invite the widows and orphans to our conference. The leaders made notes of any needs such as food, medical care, blankets or a mattress. We learned that many widows were young, having been widowed because of health issues, violence or famine. Realizing we could quickly provide for some of the needs, our church purchased more than four hundred mattresses to give to the widows.

Soon it was my turn to speak to the women. The music finally stopped, and I stepped up on stage. Looking into a sea of stunning black eyes, I assessed the group and found my heart pounding with love. What could I possibly say to breathe life or a nugget of hope into their situations? Each one had a story. I wished I had a year to sit down and hear all of them. Still staring at their eager faces, I prayed that I could encourage them as much as they had inspired me.

I began to share with them the love of Jesus. Through a translator, I spoke, "His arms were stretched wide on the cross, saying come to me. He gave the biggest bear hug the world has ever experienced, and that bear hug included you. He loved you on the cross and wants to be close to you now." I never imagined what happened next. As I stood there, they flooded the stage, kneeling humbly with tearful prayers. Many prayed the prayer of salvation to receive a "Jesus' bear hug" - the forever love He offered them. This group of hungry women were ready for transformation - not the kind of change the world has to offer but sheer salvation of the eternal, heavenly kind.

"IN THE SAME WAY, THERE IS JOY IN
THE PRESENCE OF GOD'S ANGELS
WHEN EVEN ONE SINNER REPENTS."
Luke 15:10

Do you need a bear hug from Jesus? Are you ready to put your faith in Him? Is He your source of joy? If not, I encourage you to change that today. Better yet, do it right now! I invite you to pray with me. Here's the same prayer I prayed with dozens upon dozens of African women and Kenyan children. Similar to my first prayer at the little church in town while I sat next to my friend Rhea. Join me.

> Dear Jesus,
>
> I come to You today as a child. I bow my head in thanksgiving that You came for me and You died on a cross for all my sins. Please forgive me for all my wrongdoing. I invite You into my heart to be my friend and leader forever. I am grateful that I have a secure home in heaven and even the angels rejoice today as I pray. I'm falling in love with You and look forward to building a life with You at the center.
>
> Amen.

What if you chose to take this season of your life to develop the fruit of joy? Unlike so many of the gifts God gives us through the power of His Holy Spirit, fruit is one we must grow. Fruits of the Spirit are sweet and to be enjoyed. At the same time, we must take responsibility and choose to develop and grow them until they become part of our character. Joy is a personal trait that can be embedded in your heart and shown as an example to others, but it must be yours first. Only a life with Jesus can promise everlasting joy. There is no better place to experience the fullness of joy than in His presence.

ONLY A LIFE WITH JESUS CAN PROMISE EVERLASTING JOY. THERE IS NO BETTER PLACE TO EXPERIENCE THE FULLNESS OF JOY THAN IN HIS PRESENCE.

Let us continue training ourselves in this discipline of cultivating joy and spending time with the trustworthy source of joy in our lives: Jesus.

REFLECT
choose one or two questions

Whether on your own or in a community of others, ask these questions and apply them to your life.

- What aspect of creation brings you the most joy? Flowers, trees, water or animals? Which one? When did you first realize this was life giving to you?

- What is your favorite fruit? Have you ever had a fruit tree?

- Have you ever been on a mission trip? Where did you go, and what did you do?

- Share about a childhood encounter you had with the Lord.

PRAY
this sentence prayer aloud as a group

Dear God,
Show me your love in creation and fill me with childlike faith. I receive the joy you designed for me.
Amen.

READ John 15:1-17

at least the first two paragraphs together

I am the true vine, and my Father is the gardener. He cuts off every branch in me that bears no fruit, while every branch that does bear fruit he prunes so that it will be even more fruitful. You are already clean because of the word I have spoken to you. Remain in me, as I also remain in you. No branch can bear fruit by itself; it must remain in the vine. Neither can you bear fruit unless you remain in me.

I am the vine; you are the branches. If you remain in me and I in you, you will bear much fruit; apart from me you can do nothing. If you do not remain in me, you are like a branch that is thrown away and withers; such branches are picked up, thrown into the fire and burned. If you remain in me and my words remain in you, ask whatever you wish, and it will be done for you. This is to my Father's glory, that you bear much fruit, showing yourselves to be my disciples.

As the Father has loved me, so have I loved you. Now remain in my love. If you keep my commands, you will remain in my love, just as I have kept my Father's commands and remain in his love. I have told you this so that my joy may be in you and that your joy may be complete. My command is this: Love each other as I have loved you. Greater love has no one than this: to lay down one's life for one's friends. You are my friends if you do what I command. I no longer call you servants, because a servant does not know his master's business. Instead, I have called you friends, for everything that I learned from my Father I have made known to you. You did not choose me, but I chose you and appointed you so that you might go and bear fruit—fruit that will last—and so that whatever you ask in my name the Father will give you. This is my command: Love each other.

CONNECTION

Answer these questions together

Jesus gives us several commands in this passage. List them in your journal, or share them aloud. Which command do you sense God's Spirit directing you to take up from this context? Ask yourself, am I willing to follow His direction?
In verse 11, Jesus talks about joy. How does that verse inspire you?

If Jesus loves us as much as He says He does, then why do you think He has to cut off the unfruitful branches? Why is it so difficult? What branches in your life need pruning? How does that make you feel? What is the benefit? Explain.

Who is the gardener? Who is the vine? Who are we?
Jesus mentions another fruit of the Spirit, love. Jesus establishes love as integral to this new way of living. How does loving God and loving others enable joy to flow freely in our lives?

In Psalm 51:11-12, David prays, "Do not cast me from your presence or take your Holy Spirit from me. Restore to me the joy of your salvation and grant me a willing spirit to sustain me." David knows that the source of his joy is his connection with God through the Holy Spirit. Share your salvation experience. Describe the joy you felt. What would it take to renew that in your life today?

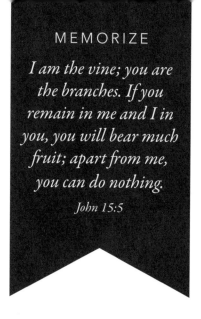

PRAYER POINTS

Does anyone in the group want to receive Jesus as Savior today?

Let's recommit our hearts and lives to connect with Him this week.

GROUP CHALLENGE

One winter day, I hiked with a friend to photograph a rare sighting of the Snowy Owl. How can you spend some extended time in nature this week? (What will you do? Hike, garden or snow ski?) Describe the refreshment it brings.

Recipe Idea - At the end of each chapter you will find a recipe. Make one of these to share with your family or small group.

GROUP ACTIVITY

Visit a local zoo.
Where do you find joy in God's creation?

Journal
AT HOME

Picture yourself at the moment of your salvation. Describe the experience.

How can you keep the joy of salvation? Write any ideas or changes you desire to make to cultivate that fruit. If you have never welcomed Jesus into your life as Savior, consider doing this now and journal your time with the Lord.

TOMATO, BASIL & MOZZARELLA SALAD

INGREDIENTS

Salad

Cherry tomatoes

1 bunch fresh Basil

1 fresh mozzarella ball

Dessing

Balsamic vinegar

Olive Oil

Salt and pepper

I like to use the carton of tomatoes with the mixed colors of red and yellow, but any will do

DIRECTIONS

Wash and cut the tomatoes in half and place in a salad bowl. Chop and add the mozzarella ball into small bite size pieces. Take scissors and cut thin strips of the basil on top to taste. I like lots of Basil so use 4-5 leaves for a small carton of tomatoes.

Drizzle olive oil and balsamic vinegar on top with salt and pepper. Toss and serve with crusty bread or grilled chicken.

CHAPTER

2

Joy in the Presence of Jesus

"You make known to me the path of life; you will fill me with joy in your presence, with eternal pleasures at your right hand" (Psalm 16:11).

"Surely you have granted him unending blessings and made him glad with the joy of your presence" (Psalm 21:6).

At the end of one already long workday, I had a scheduled Zoom call. Quickly brushing my hair and teeth with the hopes of appearing presentable from the neck up, I was ready to start the meeting. The online waiting room had women prepared to join, pray and study the Bible together. All of a sudden, I realized that my computer was almost out of battery. Ugh! I scrambled for an extension cord, quickly plugging it in near my desk. Whew, that was a close one!

Do you know that feeling? Have you ever panicked because your phone or computer was about to die? I simply had not stopped long enough to ensure my laptop had sufficient battery to make it through the evening. The same thing happens to us spiritually when we busy ourselves to the point of no return. Failing to spend daily time with Jesus zaps us of our joy. When my day is completely packed and void of time in His presence, it never fails that I end up rushing and frustrated. I'm quickly out of step with God's Holy Spirit and His subsequent gentle nudges that point me in the right direction.

It's easy to do. I can flat-out become sidetracked from my true priorities. The reminder bell rings when I feel tension, hurry or stress rising within me. When our boys were little, they would ask, "Mommy, what are we going to do today?" They taught me to approach the Lord with child-like faith and ask Him, "Lord Jesus, what is your plan for the day?" Learning to start my day with Jesus, spend portions of the middle of my day with Him, and quiet my Spirit alongside Him as the day comes to a close is the most fulfilling and rewarding way of life. Easier said than done, I know. But, yes, there is a conscious decision each day about our time and how to spend it. Will we venture off on our own and assume that He will follow where we lead? Or will we plug into the source and allow His Spirit to direct every step of our days?

CONNECTING TO THE SOURCE IS NOT SIMPLY LIVING LIFE WITH A COMPASS; INSTEAD, STAYING CONNECTED TO THE SOURCE IS VITAL BECAUSE IT ALLOWS US TO LIVE LIFE TO THE FULLEST.

"Jesus said: I say these things so that you may have the full measure of my joy within" (John 17:13).

Remember Tigger the Tiger from Winnie the Pooh? Bounding with energy and jumping for joy, He was the complete opposite of Eeyore, who lived a negative and depressing existence. While Tigger and Eeyore are extreme examples, the temptation to live like Eeyore is much greater and more pervasive throughout our world than the temptation to live like Tigger. It's easy to get discouraged, isn't it? And it's no wonder. We have a strong enemy named Satan, and he and his minions roam the earth trying to distract us from living a life filled with God's love and joy.

Jesus warned us that Satan would try his best to steal and destroy our lives, but also, Jesus does not want us to live in fear. Instead, Jesus encourages us to stay vigilant and on guard. Satan aims to harass us with despair and a loss of confidence, but he doesn't get to win. The good news is that we have access to Jesus, and Jesus already won the battle for us. He promises to give us His presence and fill us to overflowing with HIs joy.

Back to Tigger and Eeyore. We get to choose who we want to be. Do you want to be like Tigger, full of life and joy? Or do you want to live like Eeyore, always living from a place of defeat? Because of Jesus' renewable source of joy in our lives, we can live a Tigger life (or at the very least, more Tigger and less Eeyore). Let us plug into that source again and again and again, and let us anticipate the promised outcome: a life of joy.

Are you jumping yet?

"The thief comes only to steal and kill and destroy; I have come that they may have life and have it to the full" (John 10:10).

Joy as a Team in His Presence

Bump, bump bump as we hit the potholes on an African country drive. The landscape is lush with endless green as we pass rows of corn in farmers' fields. I see gardens, a couple of goats, lots of chickens and an occasional cow. The sky is expansive as far as the eye can see, the weather is a thick balmy heat, and my heart is full of joy.

Packed like sardines in the air-conditioned car (thank goodness for the air conditioning!), we are on our way to an orphanage. Riding along with our team is Bishop Evans Achanga and his dynamic wife Mellen.

Evans is a kind, powerful and wise leader, and he oversees more than 150 churches dotted all over Kenya, with some in Tanzania and Sudan. He and Mellen are on fire for Jesus, and they are among my most dear and respected friends.

As we drive, we sing. As we drive, we burst into prayer. We mix singing, prayer and thanksgiving to God for the entire three hours toward our orphanage, which sits nestled near the base of Mt Kilimanjaro, the tallest mountain in the world. I look out the window and see women carrying heavy, giant, yellow water jugs on their heads. With their children in tow, the women use both hands to steady the weight of the enormous jugs. I whisper a prayer, asking God to send these women to our conferences so that we might be able to offer them food, medicine and the love of Jesus.

I pray for the children. "God, would You fill our orphanage with practical help like electricity and furniture but most importantly for amazing parents who will care for these kids?" While praying, tears easily fall, and I sense His goodness around me. I feel that God's heart is close to these prayers, so I add more. God and I are in a conversation about something that matters most to Him - His people. As I pray quietly in my cocoon by the car window, the others continue to chat and sing. The car is full of God's love.

Then, suddenly surprised, we all scream in amazement, "Look!" There along the road is an impressive family of the most spectacular giraffes I have ever seen. I think to myself, "If He cares for baby giraffes, then for sure He hears our prayers for the sweet little ones who will fill the orphanage home one day. I know He will take care of them." When we ask, when we sing, when we seek, and when we knock, He is there. He wants to be with us. The Lord is near.

"For everyone who asks receives; the one who seeks finds; and to the one who knocks, the door will be opened" (Matthew 7:8).

"True spirituality that is pure in the eyes of our Father God is to make a difference in the lives of the orphans, and widows in their troubles, and to refuse to be corrupted by the world's values" (James 1:27 TPT).

Hurdles To Joy

When I returned home from our trip, I had the nagging thought, "Why can't His presence be experienced more and more in my life each day? Isn't God the same here as He is around the world? How can I access the joy of the Lord - the happy contentment that I encountered on the bumpy car ride in Kenya - here and now at home?" The path toward joy with Jesus is simple, yet we face many untruths that keep us from a more profound experience of Him.

> THE PATH TOWARD JOY WITH JESUS IS SIMPLE, YET WE FACE MANY UNTRUTHS THAT KEEP US FROM A MORE PROFOUND EXPERIENCE OF HIM.

I used to find myself trapped in obstacles that kept me from the complete joy found in Jesus. One of the first hurdles in staying connected to the source is overcoming the obstacles that prevent us from doing so. First, we must take time to identify any lie that keeps us from quality time with Jesus.

Before we address some of the common lies that keep us from spending time with the source of joy, let's clear our hearts in prayer. Join me.

Dear Jesus,

You are my savior, friend and king. I come today and just want to say I apologize. I need Your forgiveness for failing to spend time with You. I know You love me and want to enjoy me. I know that there is joy in Your presence. I want to be close to You too.

Amen.

Now let us unravel any lies we may be hearing that keep us from the presence of Jesus.

The first hurdle is obedience: *I don't have enough hours in the day to spend time with Jesus.* It is challenging. We all have the same twenty-four hours, yet how we spend those hours is a minute-by-minute decision. A breakthrough came for me when I realized that "my time" was not "my time." My time is His time. My time belongs to the Lord. Welcoming God's leading voice and His advice into every moment of my life was a game-changer.

The second hurdle is self: *If I spend time with Him, it might be boring or wasteful.* If you are like me, you keep a running to-do list. I don't understand the concept of being bored. There are a million demands on my time at the office, and there are never-ending chores at home. When I'm not working on my work list or my house list, I have people to see, places to go and things to do. I daydream about having extra time to decorate, entertain, read or bake. The concept of spending time with Jesus often seems like a good idea once everything else is "done." Work is never done. Gee whiz - that's the problem. I learned that time with Jesus is exciting, the complete opposite of boring. He can be part of my work and my play. I even long for more of Him after spending hours sitting in His presence. Connection with Him is directional, not wasteful. When I prioritize time with Jesus, I save myself time and find myself with more energy. He is worth every minute.

The third hurdle is relational follow-through: *To be with Jesus, I have to sacrifice or give up something I want.* I didn't realize that by believing this lie, I was losing precious time in my day because I was away from the source of my life. I was away from the director and therefore wasted valuable time on things outside of His will.

Nurturing Joy

Spending time with Jesus can be part of your routine. Intentional changes with focus and commitment have made all the difference in my life. At first, you may think this is checkbox living, but God invites us to take Him off our "to do" list and to simply be, simply be with Him. By choosing to include Him in a daily plan or commitment, we give Him the freedom to move with us throughout our day. Over time you will see the closeness experienced, the foundation of godliness built on His Word, and the love for Him formed in your heart.

GOD INVITES US TO TAKE HIM OFF OUR "TO DO" LIST AND SIMPLY BE WITH HIM.

Practically, many good habits formed as I shifted my mindset from "my time" to "His time."

First, I love to commit to a time and place. I think of this as I would coffee with a close friend. Having a chair with a basket of pens, paper and my Bible is critical for me. I desperately try to arrive at the same time every morning, light a candle and spend some time with my source of neverending joy, coffee in hand. I realize this changes depending on the season of life. When I was up all night with two babies under two, the times would flex. When I stayed up until 2:00 a.m. talking with a teenager, the time and place would move. When I was exhausted from working all week and then hosting a women's event all weekend, I would crave, cherish and guard this time as I ran to my Father for restoration. I like to change things around; no day or week is ever the same for me, and I have learned that is ok. I hope that as you read this you are pondering your style and responsibilities because I'm a firm believer that when we lay our lives at His feet, He supernaturally helps us. He will grant us, afford us and help us carve out time to be with Him.

On a practical note, I like to read through the Bible with a book-mark so I can see where I've been and where I'm heading. I always write prayers in my journal. I love to pour out my heart to the Lord in writing where somehow I open up and share at a deeper level. Sometimes I sit quietly, simply listening in stillness during our entire time together. I ask the Lord in prayer to show me and prompt me in the areas He wants me to change. I pray about the schedule for the day, week and even farther ahead. I like to ask Him, What do you think about this? Should we go here or there? Should we do this or that? I tell him the dreams and visions I see, and instead of assuming, I listen and wait. Including Him in decisions is critical. I watch and wait for His response to me through His word, prayer or people. Jesus is our real example be-cause scripture tells us repeatedly that He "withdrew" to be with His father. He went to the mountains, went early, and scripture even says that He went to lonely places. I wonder if He felt lonely and needed time with God or if the site was simply quiet and vacant so He could think and pray? If Jesus needed this time for comfort, direction, and prayer, why would we need it any less?

"But Jesus often withdrew to lonely places and prayed" (Luke 5:16).

"Now listen, you who say, 'Today or tomorrow we will go to this or that city, spend a year there, carry on business and make money.' Why you do not even know what will happen tomorrow. What is your life? You are a mist that appears for a little while and then vanishes" (James 4:13-14).

Taking time to be grateful for the people, provisions and answers I see in my life is another way I enjoy the Father regularly. Worship is also a way to connect with God, but I usually save musical worship for the shower, daily chores or driving. I love to listen and participate in the music through singing to express my heart in worship. Praise is a foundational step in building our faith. Rotating these disciplines in complete abandon and freedom is vital because God is personal, and we are in a relationship.

Time with God is similar to the many things I like to do with my husband. We go out to eat, we watch movies together, we work on our mini-farm together, we serve God together, and we pray together. We are partners. Each day is different. There is give and take because it is a relationship. We also tell one another that we love each other or go on long drives to talk about stressful or serious issues. When we are dependent upon Jesus and Father God, it is comparable in that our relationship includes diverse experiences.

There are multiple ways we can lean on Jesus. Ask God to give you a picture, a dream or a vision, and see what He shows you. We are currently remodeling an old farmhouse. It is challenging to figure out how to put in a bathroom with minimal space on a tight budget, so I took it to God in prayer. Then one morning, I had a clear picture of my Granny Hazel's farm bathroom. I saw the pink laundry hamper under the window and the lace curtains blowing in the breeze overlooking her grapevines. I saw the tiered shelf holding towels and Mary Kay cosmetics in the corner of the small bathroom. I could even smell her floral shampoo. That picture gave me the precise idea of what I wanted for our farmhouse bathroom. I knew it was a wink from God. I knew the memory of Granny Hazel's bathroom was from the Lord. Thank you, Lord.

Here are a few of the many ways you can begin to incorporate His presence throughout your day.

- Journaling
- Listening through solitude and silence
- Reading His word
- Praying in the Holy Spirit
- Reading christian books
- Offering thanks and praise
- Participating in worship
- Offering verbal declarations of His promises
- Prayer ("mini' prayers, written prayers, church prayers, extended times of prayer)
- Setting a timer on your phone to stop and seek God for guidance

The unique ways in which we can meet with God are endless because He is an infinitely creative and ever-present God. Isn't it wonderful that we can connect with the source of true joy at any moment, no matter the circumstance?

Moses and the Presence of God

One of the greatest examples of spending time uniquely with the Lord is found in scripture. Moses was a faithful man who walked with God, even retreating far atop a mountain to be with Him. Scripture tells us that, "when Moses came down from Mount Sinai with the two tablets of the covenant law in his hands, he was not aware that his face was radiant because he had spoken with the Lord" (Exodus 14:29). In fact Moses wore a veil over his face because the radiating glow was so intense.

Isn't that what we want? To be radiating with so much joy after spending time in God's presence that others are nearly blinded by our joyful radiance?

What I love about Moses is that he was an ordinary man. He was insecure and weighed down by the problems in his life. As a result of his struggles, he learned how to communicate intimately with the Lord, and as a result of that, he lived a life of joy-filled faith.

Moses carried the weight of wholehearted devotion to God while making a difference for an entire nation. Put yourself in Moses' sandals. He had deep love and compassion for his suffering Hebrew people. He must have been burdened by the hard heart of his adoptive father, Pharaoh. Moses was grief-stricken when he came down from the mountain and discovered that the Israelites were worshipping foreign gods. Over the years, there were many times when Moses had opportunities to turn to God, and he did. Moses sought the Lord continually throughout his complicated life. God continually redeemed Moses' situation, and He will do the same for you and me.

GOD CONTINUALLY REDEEMED MOSES' SITUATION, AND HE WILL DO THE SAME FOR YOU AND ME.

God gave Moses the gift of extended time in the wilderness with a lovely new wife, a phenomenal father-in-law and two young boys. God helped Moses by providing him with his brother Aaron and sister Miriam, and together they led the people through the Red Sea. God provided not once but repeatedly for Moses and the Israelites. He guided them through the Ten Commandments and restored their health through miraculous healings. He showered them with manna from heaven. God was faithful. Moses walked through life with faith, remaining close to the Lord even when it was not easy and even when God asked him to do things he did not want to do. God expected and entrusted Moses to lead, speak and help God's people, and ultimately Moses did precisely that.

Despite Moses' lack of confidence, God believed in Moses, and God believes in you.

"The Lord would speak to Moses face to face as one speaks to a friend" (Exodus 33:11).

"With him, I speak face to face, clearly and not in riddles; he sees the form of the Lord" (Numbers 12:8).

God's character is consistent. The faithful and dependable God of Moses is the same God we know today. He desires to be close to us, and He longs for us to spend time with Him. Moses demonstrated how to experience the fullness of God by staying close to Him. Moses teaches us to respond to God in humility and obedience. In return, we see Moses as a man of faith and a man of great joy. Time and again, he led God's people in celebration, victory and song. Exodus 15, Deuteronomy 32 and Psalm 90 are three of the songs that Moses wrote, and they teach us how to declare the goodness and joy of the Lord no matter the circumstances that we face.

When Pharaoh's horses, chariots and charioteers rushed into the sea, the Lord caused them to be engulfed by the water. But the people of Israel walked through the middle of the sea on dry ground! After the Lord brought Moses and the people through the Red Sea, Moses led the people in worship:

GOD'S CHARACTER IS CONSISTENT. THE FAITHFUL AND DEPENDABLE GOD OF MOSES IS THE SAME GOD WE KNOW TODAY.

"I will sing to the Lord, for he has triumphed gloriously; he has hurled both horse and rider into the sea. The Lord is my strength and my song; he has given me victory. This is my God, and I will praise him— my father's God, and I will exalt him! The Lord is a warrior; Yahweh is his name!

"Who is like you among the gods, O Lord— glorious in holiness, awesome in splendor, performing great wonders? You raised your right hand, and the earth swallowed our enemies. "With your unfailing love you lead the people you have redeemed. In your might, you guide them to your sacred home.

"The Lord will reign forever and ever!"
(Portions of Exodus 15:1-19 NLT)

After the Lord gave Moses instructions for the Ten Commandments, Moses responded in worship and song:

"Listen, O heavens, and I will speak! Hear, O earth, the words that I say! Let my teaching fall on you like rain; let my speech settle like dew. Let my words fall like rain on tender grass, like gentle showers on young plants. I will proclaim the name of the Lord; how glorious is our God! He is the Rock; his deeds are perfect. Everything he does is just and fair. He is a faithful God who does no wrong; how just and upright he is!" (Deuteronomy 32:1-4 NLT)

"Rejoice with him, you heavens, and let all of God's angels worship him. Rejoice with his people, you Gentiles, and let all the angels be strengthened in him" (Deuteronomy 32:43a NLT).

Moses was a joyous and faithful leader. He kept his eyes on the next generation, and he lived life in light of eternity. His joy, faith and eternal perspective are reflected in the songs that he wrote, sang and shared with the people of God.

"Satisfy us in the morning with your unfailing love that we may sing for joy and be glad all our days. Make us glad for as many days as you have afflicted us, for as many years as we have seen trouble. May your deeds be shown to your servants, your splendor to their children" (Psalm 90:14-16).

From Moses, we learn to recognize and celebrate God's victory in our lives. Moses used the gift of song to lead God's people in worship and praise, thanking God for all He did in their lives. Moses' recorded songs are beautiful examples of the fruit of joy that overflowed from his life. As Moses remained close to God, the source of perfect, everlasting joy, Moses shared the joy of the Lord with the Israelites. Moses led the people forward as a cheerleader by celebrating the victories and giving thanks even in hard times. Likewise, we can lead others in joy by remaining close to God's presence and acknowledging His goodness in our lives.

Consider the ways that you can lead others in joy. What can you add to this list?

- Share in the song. Lead others in song and victory!
- Accept His call by choosing obedience. Go in boldness where God sends you.
- Humbly share God's presence and communicate with Him in humility.
- Trust the results. Believe in God for great things: provisions, directions, miracles and deliverances.

Moses had so much in his life to overwhelm him - Hebrew adoption, identity insecurity, rejection by Pharaoh, ten plagues, crossing the Red Sea, making a murderous mistake and a burning bush. But Moses remained faithful to God despite how crushing his circumstances were. As a result, Moses lived a life of obedience, faith and joy. In the same way, we live a life of faith and joy by remaining close to Jesus, no matter how overwhelming life can be. Let Him overwhelm you with His presence. You may be mind-boggled and tired of all the demands or difficulties. Pause. Breathe. And let Him amaze you with his love. Immerse yourself in His presence, and let joy flow.

Discussion Guide

REFLECT
choose one or two questions

Whether on your own or in a community of others, ask these questions and apply them to your life.

- What is the first home you remember? Describe living there. Did you share a bedroom?

- Who is the wisest person you know? How did you get to know them? How did they learn wisdom?

- What was your first job outside your family home? What did you learn from that experience?

- We have been talking about joy. When was your last joy-filled moment? What went into that experience?

PRAY
this sentence prayer aloud as a group

Dear God,
I bow my heart in love and awe of You. Give me instructions for today. I praise you for your incredible power working in my life.
Amen.

 # READ

EXODUS 15:1-6, 10-13 NLT

I will sing to the Lord, for he has triumphed gloriously; he has hurled both horse and rider into the sea. The Lord is my strength and my song; he has given me victory. This is my God, and I will praise him— my father's God, and I will exalt him! The Lord is a warrior; Yahweh is his name! Pharaoh's chariots and army he has hurled into the sea. The finest of Pharaoh's officers drowned in the Red Sea. The deep waters gushed over them; they sank to the bottom like a stone. Your right hand, O Lord, is glorious in power. Your right hand, O Lord, smashes the enemy.

But you blew with your breath, and the sea covered them. They sank like lead in the mighty waters. Who is like you among the gods, O Lord— glorious in holiness, awesome in splendor, performing great wonders? You raised your right hand, and the earth swallowed our enemies. With your unfailing love you lead the people you have redeemed. In your might, you guide them to your sacred home.

PSALM 90:3-6, 14-17

You turn people back to dust, saying, "Return to dust, you mortals." A thousand years in your sight are like a day that has just gone by, or like a watch in the night. Yet you sweep people away in the sleep of death— they are like the new grass of the morning. In the morning, it springs up new, but by evening it is dry and withered.

Satisfy us in the morning with your unfailing love, that we may sing for joy and be glad all our days. Make us glad for as many days as you have afflicted us, for as many years as we have seen trouble. May your deeds be shown to your servants, your splendor to their children. May the favor of the Lord our God rest on us; establish the work of our hands for us— yes, establish the work of our hands.

CONNECTION
Answer these questions together

Read Exodus 15: 1-6. Have you thanked and acknowledged God for a narrow escape in your life? When? What happened?

Read Psalm 90:3-6. Moses explains that life is brief. How does that reality change the way you think about or live for God?

Moses faced many insecurities and rejections. Share with the group some of the similarities or differences you have with Moses.

Earlier in this chapter, Jennifer mentions three hurdles that can keep us from God:
- Obedience
- Self
- Relational follow-through

What stumbling block can you relate to the most?

Read Psalm 90:14-17. How has God intervened in your life when you were overwhelmed? How do you express joy?

How would you like to change or improve your current patterns of connecting with God? Describe your routines for connecting with Jesus.

Read Exodus 15:10-13. Can you see how Moses details the hand of God? Is worship a solid foundation for you? How can you incorporate more praise and worship daily? What would you have to stop doing to have space to add worship?

PRAYER POINTS

WORSHIP God with a physical response in prayer (bow your head, physically kneel, open your hands up or lift your hands before Him).

Praise God in prayer for WHO He is (provider, mighty, king, comforter).

Thank God in prayer for WHAT he has done for you (salvation, help, healing, deliverance).

GROUP CHALLENGE

Intentionally listen to music and worship with your children or grandchildren while cooking or baking. Then, try one of the recipes in this book!

GROUP ACTIVITY

Invite a friend or two or perhaps your entire group to spend extended time at your house in prayer and connection with God.

Journal
AT HOME

Journal your history with God. Write about your God highlights.

When do you remember first meeting God? What are some of the God milestones in your life? Make a list of all the times He has "parted the Red Sea" for you. Thank Him for moments in your life when He showed up for you. Consider including these dates and stories in your Bible as a memorial for future generations.

EASY ICE CREAM SUNDAES

Years ago when I was a pre-school mom, my next-door neighbor Laura gave me this recipe and I have used it for years. It is fun and easy and everyone loves it. Also, it will last a long time in your freezer but ours is usually eaten quickly! This is perfect for a summer birthday or holiday party.

INGREDIENTS

1 package of classic Oreos

1 stick of butter

1 half-gallon of vanilla ice cream (I usually get the cheapest)

1 container of salted peanuts

1 jar of hot fudge sauce

1 jar of caramel sauce (optional)

1 container of creamy cool whip

1 jar of Marcheno cherries

DIRECTIONS

1. Set your ice cream and cool whip on the counter to soften.

2. Meanwhile, open your stick of butter partially and grease a 9x14" glass pan.

3. Melt remaining butter in the microwave.

4. Crush the entire package of Oreos. *(I do this in a large zip lock back with my hands and a rolling pin, no need to be crushed extra-fine, lumpy is ok)*

5. In a bowl stir and coat the Oreos with your melted butter and spread into the bottom of the glass pan.

6. Spread the softened vanilla ice cream over the Oreo crust.

7. Sprinkle a layer of salty peanuts on top of the ice cream. I like to press a few down into the ice cream.

8. Spread your hot fudge sauce on top of the peanuts. *(you may need to microwave a few seconds for it to be spreadable)*

9. Spread your cool whip layer on top.

10. Depending on the size of your pieces, I usually get at least 12 nice square pieces from this desert. Place a cherry from the jar where you will cut each piece.

11. Cover tightly with saran wrap and freeze overnight.

CHAPTER

2

Joy in Relationships

Despite a long work week, a messy house and a pile of homework the boys needed to finish, I had a strong feeling in my gut that we needed to visit my grandma. After giving myself a pep talk that the rest, clean house and math worksheets could wait, we packed and loaded up for the three-hour drive to Kentucky where my grandma lived.

During our drive, I felt the emotional weight of our visit. When we made a pit stop for chocolate milkshakes (the boys' favorite), I could hardly eat as I fought back the tears that were brimming at the surface of my eyes. Hoping to settle my emotions, I ran into a nearby pharmacy to pick up a few things for Grandma. I bought a hairbrush, a bright fleece pink blanket decorated with butterflies and a pack of Freedent gum, her favorite. Carrying the bag of gifts, I thought, "Could this possibly be our last time together?" My mind and heart raced with fond memories of my beloved grandma, and I imagined what I might say to her that would bring her a smile, gratitude or encouragement.

You see, my grandma was simply the best. She was an all-American grandma who adored us, and she often expressed her love to us with her homemade apple pie, fried chicken and garden-fresh vegetables. She cherished us beyond words, and I adored her. Her white ranch nestled on forty acres of beautiful farmland and tobacco fields. I thought that her one thousand square foot house was perfect. In the spring, her gardens bloomed with flowers, and the pasture brimmed bright with yellow daffodils. Her dancing blue eyes matched the pale blue gingham plaid shirt she often wore with a crisply ironed khaki skirt. She always looked so lovely. At church, she was an example of what it is to give and serve. She generously invested in my life, teaching me right from wrong and the value of honesty.

When I was a little girl, she grabbed a basket and my hand, and together we walked to the edge of the farm to pick wild blackberries, skipping and talking all the way. Then, back in the kitchen, she taught me the simple delight of sugar sprinkled atop fresh-picked berries. When I became a mom, she loved my boys and found immeasurable joy and pleasure in our new family. I talked with her unreservedly, and she always helped me find suitable and peace-filled answers to my many questions about life, marriage and motherhood.

How could I say goodbye to someone I found such deep love and comfort connecting with throughout my entire life?

When we arrived at Grandma's, Doyle offered to keep the boys busy so that I could have time alone with her. I geared up and rushed in, and we greeted each other with our typical loud and exuberant greetings. "Hey, Hey, Hey, Grandma! Oh my goodness, It's so good to see you!" She sat up in bed and grinned from ear to ear, "Hey, Hey, Hey, How are you? Where are the boys?"

"They are coming in a little bit, and they can't wait to see you, Grandma. I brought you a soft blanket, and I thought I would brush your hair."

Always a comforter, Grandma responded, "Why don't you just get up here in the bed with me?"

HOW COULD I SAY GOODBYE TO SOMEONE I FOUND SUCH A DEEP LOVE AND COMFORT CONNECTING WITH THROUGHOUT MY ENTIRE LIFE?

As I climbed in, I took pictures in my mind of her famous blue eyes highlighted by her matching light blue gown. We chatted non-stop while I brushed her hair. Then, almost as if she knew this short time together was a lasting one, she pulled my head cozily into her chest and held it there with her hands in a long snuggle that only a grandma can give. Her warm embrace combined with the scent of Oil of Olay was like a promise to my heart that we would one day be together again in heaven. In that forever moment, she spoke over me the most simple words which fueled my needy soul. She said, "Jenny, to me, in my heart, you will always be my little girl with blonde pigtails playing under my apple tree on the farm."

My grandma was pure joy and pure love.

You might think I cried the entire way home that day, but instead, my heart was full. Is this joy I feel as I remember all of our times together? I think it is. A few short weeks after that visit, Grandma passed into eternity with a hearty welcome from Jesus, whom she honored and served throughout her entire life. Even now, I still find myself combing through all the lessons of character and connection that she taught me and the endless gifts that she instilled in my life.

Jesus-Centered Connection Fuels Joy

A relational connection that is centered around Jesus fuels true joy. Just like the trinity - Father, Son and Holy Spirit, we too are designed for relationships. It is through our relationships that we can find and spread joy.

God is relational. It is hard to imagine, but our creative God of the universe, Abraham, Isaac, and Jacob, is a personal, relational God. He waits for us. He longs to commune with us. He pursues us with His love, all the while inviting us to spend time with Him and others. God loved us so much that He knew there must be a real solution to the sin and evil that puts a barrier between Him and us in this fallen world. His answer is so powerful that it allows us to know and fellowship with Him in an intimate and practical, daily living kind of way. He desperately wanted a final solution that would place us in complete unity with Him. His plan was a relationship. His plan was Christ.

REGARDLESS OF HOW WE CONNECT WITH JESUS, HE OFFERS US REAL, TANGIBLE AND FULFILLING JOY THROUGH OUR TIME SPENT WITH HIM.

"For here is the way God loved the world—he gave his only, unique Son as a gift. So now, everyone who believes in him will never perish but experience everlasting life" (John 3:16 TPT).

The cross is like a bridge. Think of walking across a bridge, from the ugly side that includes sin and death to the glorious side that provides wholeness and hope. Because of the cross, we have perfect access to fellowship and can relate to God the Father, Jesus the Son and the Holy Spirit. Each supernatural component of the "three in one" has a distinct and cherished role in our lives. As we get to know the three, Father, Son and Holy Spirit, we find companionship, courage, comfort and answers to our questions. What a priceless gift.

When I am desperate, and in need, I run to Father God for protection. It is resting in the safety and security of His hands that I find joy.

Because of our relationship with Jesus, we can know the sacrificial love of a triune God who is compassionate, tender, authentic and trustworthy. Jesus is near us no matter the difficulties. It is in that kinship that we can find joy in all seasons.

The Holy Spirit nudges us, guides and points our hearts toward God's presence and plan. The Spirit's discernment brings freedom to our lives that leads to never-ending joy.

The bottom line is that we have immediate access to the most majestic, powerful, creative, loving and forgiving team in heaven. How can it be? I will probably spend the rest of my life in awe of this certainty, and I likely will never find the words to express the extent of my gratitude fully. The benefits of the trinity bring me so much joy.

What is a Genuine, Meaningful Connection?

Despite everything we have in the trinity, there are still seasons in our lives when we feel lonely. Perhaps you have moved, changed jobs, missed out on a family gathering or lost a loved one. Maybe the circumstances in your life seem incredibly unique, causing you to feel like you are living on an island. Yet, no matter our situation, each of us can relate to feeling lonely at times.

When Doyle accepted the job as senior pastor in Columbus, the extra two hours added to the drive home to our Kentucky and Tennessee families didn't seem like a big deal. Twenty three years later, and now we fully understand the enormous sacrifice we embraced for the purpose of following God and spreading His word throughout Columbus. Many special birthdays, July Fourths, Father's Days and Christmas Eves have been spent away from our loved ones, but more than that, we have missed countless everyday moments with our precious out-of-town family and friends. Even as I write about it, I can't quite find the words to express how much we have missed them. I realize missionaries overseas live with this ache for years at a time, so why would I think I am any different? I simply acknowledge that it has been really hard. That loneliness has remained a tender spot in my heart for over two decades, and only God knows how deeply I long to be with our loved ones.

Even though we know that we always have access to God, we still long for human interaction. Lone Ranger Christianity is not the way God designed us to live. In other words, we were not meant to live a faith-filled life all alone. Instead, God wants us to live in a relationship with Him and each other. We call that community. By God's grace, we have created a vibrant faith community right here in Columbus, and we even get to experience having one of our sons and daughters-in-love live nearby. That doesn't make up for what we miss, but it has allowed us to experience the rich blessing of Jesus-centered relationships right where we are.

I also recognize that living in community - even a faith community - is not always easy. However, even when we experience pain or hurt within our community, we still need each other. Ultimately, it is through community that we also find healing. When we foster relationships with friends and family, we see ourselves clearer, both the good and the bad. Relationships refine us, like the finest grit sandpaper that smooths out our rough edges over time.

RELATIONSHIPS REFINE US, LIKE THE FINEST GRIT SANDPAPER THAT SMOOTHS OUT OUR ROUGH EDGES OVER TIME.

By including different types of people in our lives, we experience the joy of diversity. Additionally, we each enter relationships at different seasons of life, and as a result, how we love, serve and connect ebbs and flows. Your community likely includes weak people who need to be strengthened by your presence and others who support you during your moments of weakness. In a community, we carry each other, uphold each other and encourage each other. Think of your relationships like a tennis match where you have a back-and-forth exchange of challenging insights, hopeful encouragements, helpful support, excitement, fun and love. Our relationships teach us, mentor us, protect us and spur us on toward positive personal growth. We need all kinds of fellowship to make us who God intended us to be, and as we experience His plan for our relationships, we discover joy upon joy.

Through decades of ministry leadership, I learned the hard way to have positive, encouraging people in my life to bring balance as I often spent time with people who require a lot of me physically, emotionally, mentally and spiritually. Helping others is an energizing experience that God expects. He also wants us to enjoy one another, sharpen one another and together know Him. Balance is key. If we never help one another, then we become self-absorbed. If we never have positive people around us, we live drained and unable to enjoy our family. When you meet someone who pours into your life, you are forever grateful. When Jesus is at the center of the relationship, we find honest joy through being close. There is nothing like this mix - fellowship and Jesus. The excitement of joy found in any friendship where Jesus is the core is rare and should be looked for and sought after like a treasure.

THE EXCITEMENT OF JOY FOUND IN ANY RELATIONSHIP WHERE JESUS IS THE CORE IS RARE AND SHOULD BE LOOKED FOR AND SOUGHT AFTER LIKE A TREASURE.

I shared a special bond with a missionary family. Many years before I met the Achangas, I was honored to know and learn life lessons of connection from the late Bishop Steve Kabachia from Kenya. His incredible wife is named Jennifer, and they have eight children. Steve planted well over a hundred churches in West Africa and founded a pastor's training school. Many of these churches were in remote areas of Kenya. In addition, his wife Jennifer started a sewing school for women.

One day we rode a few hours together to a 20+ acre plot of land in a tiny town called Loitoktok. With the sky spreading for miles above us, we joined hands in a circle on the property. Though my heart was ready to pray, I struggled to close my eyes because I was awe-struck witnessing elephants roaming in the distance.

There near the equator, heat settled in my mouth like a thick paste. With sweat-soaked necks and eyebrows glistening under the radiating sun, my endurance waned. Just then, Steve began to sing, someone else started to dance, and before long, we were a chorus of praise together on a glorious piece of land. This spontaneous worship fueled my spirit and energized my soul. We held hands and prayed over the property as Steve described his vision of building an orphanage for sixty children from all over Kenya. They would farm for their food while growing up, and most importantly, they would learn a biblical foundation and qualities for leadership. I sensed a fire within me as I listened to Steve's vision, and I knew God was placing a call on my life to participate in building the orphanage.

Steve was a godly man with nonstop energy, and his dreams for God kept him with a constant smile. No physical lack or discomfort held him back. His grin stretched from ear to ear, and his laugh grabbed you at your gut. He oozed flawless joy! Steve passed joyfulness along to me, my husband and our boys when we traveled with him. Steve's vitality and intensity for the things of God left an indelible impression on our lives. Steve knew and taught God's word. It became a living, breathing part of who he was, which spilled over into the lives of all who encountered him. He lived to serve, lead and gather others to experience this joy that blossomed from a relationship with Jesus.

HE LIVED TO SERVE, LEAD AND GATHER OTHERS TO EXPERIENCE THIS JOY THAT BLOSSOMED FROM A RELATIONSHIP WITH JESUS.

We would be together in a very hot - and I mean an Africa kind of hot - vehicle, and Steve still had joy. We would be extremely hungry, sunburnt and itching from bug bites after outdoor meetings all day, yet Steve was still helping, caring and smiling. We would be worn, beyond tired, needing a shower and upside down because of the time change, yet Steve was still kind, steady and pleasant with a joy-filled twinkle in his eye. When most people complained or argued, Steve led with joy. He simply did not let the circumstances steal his deep well of joy.

I observed Steve time and time again, and I do not know anyone who modeled joy like Bishop Steven Kabachia modeled it. I remember saying to myself, "I want that. I want what my brother has. Is that possible?" I knew I had a measure of joy, and I was grateful for that development, but I sensed more joy rising in me. Perhaps I could experience a deeper level of this fruit, more lasting throughout the ups and downs of an average day. I desired the untouchable joy that I witnessed in my brother Steve, and I hoped to be someone who passed that joy to others, just like he did to me. Steve taught by example. He carried much responsibility with eight children, a large church and many pastors to look after, yet he led with joy. His joy was overflowing from his life as a disciple of Jesus. Bishop Steve loved God's word, His voice and sharing His love, and that love manifested as immense joy in Steve's life.

"OUR MOUTHS WERE FILLED WITH
LAUGHTER, OUR TONGUES WITH
SONGS OF JOY. THEN IT WAS SAID
AMONG THE NATIONS, 'THE LORD HAS
DONE GREAT THINGS FOR THEM."
Psalm 126:2

Steve is just one example of the power of living, leading and loving with the joy of Jesus. When Jesus is at the center, joy spills out, and like a contagious fire, everyone lights up with the sustainable pleasure of heaven. I hope to grow more into a person who lives, leads and loves with a joy that others can experience.

One Indiana Summer

Contagious joy is received and given in Jesus-centered relationships. God's faithful abundance was evident during one particular summer when my family moved to Indiana. I was eleven years old, living in a new place, and I desperately prayed that God would give me a friend.

Cornrows lined the flat field surrounding our "new to us" Indiana home. We moved from Kentucky to Indiana at the beginning of summer, and school was still three long months away. I knew no one on our rural street with only a few homes. Being a highly social child, I asked my mom to pray that I would find a friend. I desperately wanted a 6th-grade Christian playmate who was close to my age. I waited for this friend every single day.

One night I had a dream, and in that vision, a moving truck pulled down the cul de sac toward the Nelsons' empty house. A car followed suit and out bounced a happy little brown-haired girl with a few cute freckles. I awakened straight from the dream and skipped into the kitchen, announcing to my mother that I would be meeting my new friend today! I was certain that God answered my prayer.

I remember my mom trying to calm my excitement and lower my expectations in case this was a setup for disappointment. However, I could not be deterred, and I knew the Lord had given me an answer in my mind. I quickly dressed and jumped on my ten-speed bike to ride to the empty driveway anticipating what God had promised. I climbed the tree on the front lawn for a bird's eye view, and I waited. I'm not sure how long I waited, but before too long, I saw a lengthy moving van coming down the main road, slowing down, and, yes, pulling into the driveway. I watched as another car followed behind. Then, true to my mind's picture, a bouncy sixth grader with brown cropped hair, cute freckles and a smile from ear to ear popped out of the car. We were quickly acquainted, and we were both thrilled to find a friend.

While the adults unloaded boxes, we climbed the tree together, talked incessantly and shared stories. Under my breath, I thanked the Lord for not letting me down and for fulfilling the dream in my heart. The Lord answered my prayer for a friend, and so my joy was complete.

<blockquote>THE LORD ANSWERED MY PRAYER FOR A FRIEND, AND SO MY JOY WAS COMPLETE.</blockquote>

"Until now, you have not asked for anything in my name. Ask, and you will receive, and your joy will be complete" (John 16:24).

I cried for much of the six-hour drive to Tennessee, our next move as a family because I could not imagine life without this best friend. Endless time spent with her was a gift of companionship for those years in Indiana.

Much like my Indiana friend, Bishop Steve in Africa and my beloved grandma, history is full of stories of joy found in relationships. Specifically, the Bible gives us a beautiful look into the lives of many Jesus followers and how their relationships nourished joy in their lives.

Think about Mary, the mother of Jesus. She was very young and newly pregnant. I can only imagine the chatter or perhaps even gossip surrounding her situation. She surrendered to God and His plan but needed some support. So she visited her cousin Elizabeth and stayed with her for three months.

Have you ever been there? Have you given everything you can to the Lord, but you still need some human interaction as you endure the process? That is normal and biblical. God provided a friend and support for Mary, and He will give friendship to you as well. Begin to ask Him, "Lord, I need a Christian friend. Please bring someone into my life who honors you and lives a life of strong character. Open my eyes to see who they are for this season of my life. Amen."

The timing of God's answer for Mary was perfect because her cousin Elizabeth was also pregnant and understood what she was going through. Sometimes we may only have one person in life who "gets it." That's what Mary had in Elizabeth, and she was grateful. You can feel the love as Elizabeth opens the front door with a warm and heartfelt greeting to her cousin Mary. In that same moment, Jesus and John the Baptist also met for the first time with some womb-leaping acrobatics.

God wants us to experience both joy and excitement; they are twins. Life should be full of these twins as we enjoy wonder and delight, bliss and cheer, and warmth and adventure when joy is present. The Holy Spirit abides in all of these feelings, which is generally the glue that binds us in Christian love. I am impressed at how Mary hurried to meet her cousin because understanding her situation was essential to what she needed. God provided her cousin at this time. Do you have someone you cannot wait to see?

"At that time, Mary got ready and hurried to a town in the hill country of Judea, where she entered Zechariah's home and greet-ed Elizabeth. When Elizabeth heard Mary's greeting, the baby leaped in her womb, and Elizabeth was filled with the Holy Spir-it. In a loud voice, she exclaimed: 'Blessed are you among women, and blessed is the child you will bear! But why am I so favored, that the mother of my Lord should come to me? As soon as the sound of your greeting reached my ears, the baby in my womb leaped for joy.' Mary stayed with Elizabeth for about three months and then returned home" (Luke 1:39-44, 56).

What about Ruth and Naomi? They were a mother and daughter-n-love duo in a crisis. Traumatic events of losing their husbands and sons pulled them together. When we face a difficult time, we simply need someone to be with us. Naomi, the mother, was on a quest for security and provision back in her hometown. Ruth was determined to not only turn over a new leaf but also to follow God. She wanted the hope that only He could deliver. She was loyal to Naomi, and at the same time she was desperate for food, shelter and confidence in God. The two women clung together through grief and struggled together to create a new life for themselves. In the end, God provided all that they needed - a home, food, a husband for Ruth and joy at the birth of a precious baby boy.

IN THE END, GOD PROVIDED ALL THAT THEY NEEDED - A HOME, FOOD, A HUSBAND FOR RUTH AND JOY AT THE BIRTH OF A PRECIOUS BABY BOY.

"But Ruth replied, 'Don't urge me to leave you or to turn back from you. Where you go I will go, and where you stay I will stay. Your people will be my people and your God my God'" (Ruth 1:16).

What about Mary and Martha? These famous Biblical figures loved others well. We know this because they opened their home not only for Jesus but also for the disciples. They were full of hospitality and partnership. They had a brother named Lazarus, and all of them were true friends. When I think about the human side of Jesus, I realize that He also needed friends. To Jesus, these friends were a refuge. They affirmed Him and His actions, even though many outsiders considered him radical. True friends affirm our God callings, and they offer safe spaces where we can sit around the table and fellowship together. This group witnessed many miracles together, celebrated together, and of course, Mary sat, honored and listened at Jesus' feet. Together they experienced the joy of impacting the world around them in the name of Jesus.

"As Jesus and his disciples were on their way, he came to a village where a woman named Martha opened her home to him. She had a sister called Mary, who sat at the Lord's feet listening to what he said" (Luke 10:38-42).

"Now Bethany was less than two miles from Jerusalem, and many Jews had come to Martha and Mary to comfort them in the loss of their brother. When Martha heard that Jesus was coming, she went out to meet him, but Mary stayed at home" (John 11:18-20).

Paul was a man of many good friends. Some people seem to have a knack for finding the best people to surround themselves with, and that was Paul. We can all learn from him about how to pick the people who surround us. Because of his wise choices, Paul made such an incredible impact on the birth of the church. He could not have done it any other way.

Anytime we step out to do great things for God, we simply cannot go at it alone. Paul knew that he must have support, and he did. We witness his life and ministry weave in and out with Silas, Barnabas, Timothy, Titus and more. Paul and Silas were ministry partners, jail buddies and church planters. Together they shared the gospel of Jesus to many new baby churches. Another of Paul's close friends was Barnabas, a chosen favorite because his name means "son of encouragement." He sold a field to help fund the mission, and he was there when Paul needed him. He served as a cheerleader who worked alongside Paul through thick and thin and encouraged him each day.

THESE RELATIONSHIPS WERE UNITED
IN JESUS AND COMMITTED TO
GLORIFYING GOD, SO TOGETHER, THEY
EXPERIENCED HIS EVERLASTING JOY.

"Joseph, a Levite from Cyprus, whom the apostles called Barnabas (which means 'son of encouragement')" (Acts 4:36).

"Judas and Silas, who themselves were prophets, said much to encourage and strengthen the believers" (Acts 15:32).

"For we wanted to come to you—certainly I, Paul, did, again and again—but Satan blocked our way. For what is our hope, our joy, or the crown in which we will glory in the presence of our Lord Jesus when he comes? Is it not you? Indeed, you are our glory and joy" (1 Thessalonians 2:18-20).

"How can we thank God enough for you in return for all the joy we have in the presence of our God because of you?" (1 Thessalonians 3:9).

How do we find relationships that bring us joy? First, we must look around at the family God has already given to us and foster those healthy relationships. Family is valuable and irreplaceable, but we must stay within our lane and choose nontoxic time together even within a family. Forgiveness, working hard to grow closer and maturing in love can go a long way toward a joyful temperament.

Some people never move beyond family relationships, and it limits their joyous experiences in life. God designed us for fellowship, but we must look in the right places to find godly choices.

"Do not be misled: 'Bad company corrupts good character'" (1 Corinthians 15:33).

We do not get to choose our family, but we do get to choose our friends. Jesus was the perfect example. First, he had John as his number one closest friend, and then he had Peter and James in his top three. After that, the twelve disciples (minus Judas, who betrayed him) were handpicked and remained in his circle of support. From there, he had the seventy-two (sent to minister in His name) and then the crowd for whom He had compassion.

I think a solid biblical church is your first and best place to start looking for these types of healthy friendships. In Acts Chapter

Two, we see how they ate, fellowshipped and prayed together, even donating needed items to each other. Start at church. Try small groups until you find one that fits with your lifestyle and temperament. I always say to look for character, chemistry, competency, and of course, look for Christ in those you choose. Sometimes we meet friendly people but they just don't match our style or bring any joy. Finding positive people is essential. We have a wonderful young man who helps us record podcasts, and he keeps us laughing. Vince has been such a gift for me, especially in this season. Statistics say that kids laugh over two hundred times a day, but adults only laugh seven to eight times. When we are working with Vince, we laugh at least a dozen times or more. It's highly satisfying! It's a joy!

"They devoted themselves to the apostles' teaching and to fellowship, to the breaking of bread and to prayer. Everyone was filled with awe at the many wonders and signs performed by the apostles. All the believers were together and had everything in common. They sold property and possessions to give to anyone who had need. Every day they continued to meet together in the temple courts. They broke bread in their homes and ate together with glad and sincere hearts" (Acts 2:42-46).

Aside from church, I like to look for friends in settings that I enjoy, such as cooking or gardening, anything that is like-minded with my interests. I love to find a satisfying prayer group, a women's group at church, or a circle of pastors' wives. Recently I joined a health group, and we share a similar journey so it is fulfilling to me. Even in those situations, guard your heart against unhealthy people. A close friendship is different from people you are reaching out to or ministering help. Friends who bring joy should be at a similar place to you spiritually.

FRIENDS WHO BRING JOY SHOULD BE IN A SIMILAR PLACE TO YOU SPIRITUALLY.

I like to imagine it as a number line with five numbers:

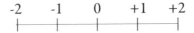

The negative twos are people who require extra time and energy from your life. You love them, help them and serve them. Negative ones are those who still require additional effort with no big deposit back into your life. Both -2's and -1's are essential to have in your life, within limitations. Jesus called us to look after each other, and that includes the negative twos and negative ones.

"The King will reply, 'Truly I tell you, whatever you did for one of the least of these brothers and sisters of mine, you did for me'" (Matthew 25:40).

Then you have the zeros. These are friends who are similar to you in spiritual maturity. I love these friends because we can freely talk about God, our family and our hobbies. In addition, zeros are healthy and foster a lot of give and take.

"Then make my joy complete by being like-minded, having the same love, being one in spirit and of one mind" (Philippians 2:2).

Positive ones are enthusiastic. They share life-giving ideas with you and offer support either spiritually or professionally. We also must have positive ones in our lives. Perhaps they help you with a project or provide you with something financially that adds value to your life. They confirm your giftings and speak hope over you. They might be the same age as you or quite possibly a decade or two older with more life experience. I once had a close friend who was ten years older than me, and she said, "Jennifer, it's ok if your friends are older than you." That helped me change my mindset about what kinds of friends I have in my life. Intentionally, I found other older friends who helped me raise kids, cook and even budget our household finances.

"Your love has given me great joy and encouragement because you, brother, have refreshed the hearts of the Lord's people" (Philemon 1:7).

Lastly, we need some positive twos in our lives. I have many. Some I have never met. They are pastors or leaders I listen to regularly. Others I have sought after or even paid for, such as our good Christian counselors. I don't see this as a weakness but as wisdom. Choose to live the principle of lifelong learning. We all need talented doctors, accountants and counselors in our lives. Each season we search and even ask positive twos to mentor us. As a follower of Jesus, we never outgrow being trained and taught. I want to be a positive person (+2), and I still need them as a learner.

As a young couple, we had a set of positive two friends who were much older than us, and they taught us about prayer. They even treated us to quality restaurants we could not afford as newlyweds. Once, they gifted us with a sparkling waterford crystal bowl and said, "You are such a fine young family, and God has a plan for your life." I still place that bowl on the center of my dining room table and remember their investment of encouragement in our lives.

"A person finds joy in giving an apt reply— and how good is a timely word" (Proverbs 15:23).

"The elder, To my dear friend Gaius, whom I love in the truth...It gave me great joy when some believers came and testified about your faithfulness to the truth, telling how you continue to walk in it. I have no greater joy than to hear that my children are walking in the truth" (3 John 1-6).

Experiencing the fruit of joy through Christ-centered relationships is one of life's greatest gifts. There is tremendous joy to be gathered in friendship. When Christ is at the center of our marriage, family or relationships, well-being follows, laughter abounds and the glory of God spills out.

REFLECT

choose one or two questions

Whether on your own or in a community of others, ask these questions and apply them to your life.

- Who was your best childhood friend? What did you do together?

- Jennifer shares about visiting her grandma for the last time. Who have you loved and lost? What was your experience the last time you were together?

- Has anyone ever modeled joy for you? Who was it, and what were they like?

PRAY

this sentence prayer aloud as a group

Dear God,
I need the right group of Christian friends. Please bring people into my life who serve You and live with solid character. Open my eyes to see them in this season of my life.
Amen.

ACTS 4:36
But you blew with your breath, and the sea covered them. TheJoseph, a Levite from Cyprus, whom the apostles called Barnabas (which means "son of encouragement").

LUKE 1:56
Mary stayed with Elizabeth for about three months and then returned home.

RUTH 1:16
But Ruth replied, "Don't urge me to leave you or to turn back from you. Where you go I will go, and where you stay I will stay. Your people will be my people and your God my God."

I CORINTHIANS 15:33
Do not be misled: "Bad company corrupts good character."

MATTHEW 25:40
The King will reply, "Truly I tell you, whatever you did for one of the least of these brothers and sisters of mine, you did for me."

CONNECTION
Answer these questions together

Even the apostle Paul needed encouragement. He has many partners and friends in the ministry. Have you ever had a "Barnabus" encourage you specifically for ministry? Which one and how?

Why do you think Mary chose to stay with Elizabeth? What did both of them need? Have you ever stayed with a family member or friend for an extended time? How did that help you?

Look at the chart. What would you rate Naomi and Ruth? Do you have -1's and -2's in your life? How are they balanced with the +1's and +2's?

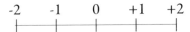

1 Corinthians 15:33 explains that bad friends can harm our good character. Have you ever experienced this? How do you effectively love your family and also protect yourself from any toxic situations? Do you pray for them?

This last verse in Matthew 25:40 is Jesus encouraging us to care for "the least of these." How can you live out this verse this week?

PRAYER POINTS

Ask God for discernment with your associations. Who should you spend your time with?

Do you need a new friend? Begin to pray about the right friendships for you.

Ask God to show you who "the least of these" are around you and how you can serve Him by loving them.

GROUP CHALLENGE

Plan a mission trip as a group. Go local. Go international. Where could you go? (Jordan's Crossing and Chavakai, Kenya opportunities are listed at www.jennifer-jackson.org).

Reach out to a potential new friend from your group this week. Invite them to lunch or coffee.

GROUP ACTIVITY

Attend something "outside the box." For example, go to a concert, retreat or ball game. Do something fun together to make a memory as a group.

Journal
AT HOME

List your closest friends, what you love about them and how grateful you are for their lives.

List any toxic people in your life. Share this with the Lord. Ask Him to show you boundaries and even elimination if needed.

ISRAELI SALAD

Israel is like a home away from home to me. We lived there as newlyweds and the mediterranean diet is certainly one of the most delicious and healthy in the world. Israelis even eat this salad for breakfast served with boiled eggs and fresh tuna fish.

This recipe is from my Mother-n-Love Betty Jackson.

INGREDIENTS

Salad

Cucumbers *(fresh and crunchy)*

Tomatoes seeded

Red, yellow or orange peppers

Cauliflower

Mild red onion

Green olives *(chopped)*

Sunflower Seeds

Feta cheese

Dried cranberries *(optional)*

Dressing

Olive oil

Vinegar *(ie. apple cider, champagne)*

Mixed herbs *(ie. Italian seasoning)*

Sugar

Fresh lemon *(optional)*

Salt

DIRECTIONS

Salad

The key with this salad is to finely chop as many crunchy vegetables as you like. You can even add broccoli as well. If you choose tomatoes I would take out the seeds to keep the salad longer in the refrig and crunchier. I only pour dressing on the amount of salad we are eating at a meal and then the veggies will last several days after the effort of chopping. We eat this all week.

Dressing

Equal parts oil/vinegar ½ cup to ½ cup with ¼ cup sugar. This creates a sweet and sour type dressing. *(If you aren't eating sugar then the cranberries add natural sweetness and use less vinegar or substitute for lemon which I love as well)*

OR: Lemon juice, olive oil and salt to taste always works *(the olives also add salt)*

CHAPTER

4

Joy in Sharing Jesus

Doyle and I climbed to the rooftop of our school on Mt Zion in Jerusalem. We needed to be alone. Overlooking the famous Kidron Valley, we ran tap water over a pregnancy test written in Hebrew. Doyle could read just enough Hebrew to understand positive or negative, and sure enough, he pieced together the block lettering to read, you guessed it - positive! As I stared at Doyle in complete shock, he eagerly said, "We must go to the Old City and get some baby moccasins lined with sheepskin. I'm so excited!"

In the Old City, we told every shop owner our good news as we searched for the perfect pair of booties. A few months later, I thought my parents would fall over when they arrived at the Israeli airport to our handmade banner proclaiming, "Welcome to Israel, Grandma and Grandpa Godbey!"

The joy I felt sharing our news was evident in my ear-to-ear smile that I simply could not wipe off my radiating face. I can still feel the profound energy that filled my veins as I reflect on those early days of discovering my first pregnancy and sharing my joy with others.

When was the last time you received some thrilling news? How did you feel upon receiving it? What was the first thing you did after you received it? If I had to guess, I bet you quickly ran to the next room or pulled out your phone to share the news with someone else.

I reflect back on those joy-filled days in Jerusalem, and I can still feel that energy and spirit of delight in my heart. But that joy is nothing compared to the joy I feel when sharing the gospel of Jesus with others.

When we share the love of Jesus with another person, we are participating in the joy of the Lord. So, likewise, when we communicate the good news of salvation, joy emerges in both our hearts and the hearts of the ones with whom we share.

There is so much joy in sharing our good news with others, and what could be better than sharing the most fantastic news of all?

Containing the gospel is impossible when it has transformed your life. What does it look like to share the joy of the good news gospel?

WHEN WE SHARE THE LOVE OF JESUS WITH ANOTHER PERSON, WE ARE PARTICIPATING IN THE JOY OF THE LORD.

Better than Kings Island

Holly and I (with five kids under age five) decided to pass the time with a special treat - a day at Kings Island, an amusement park in southwestern Ohio. Sweat and sunscreen dripped down our necks while the kids were hyped and ready for the Floom Zoom water ride. Our husbands were out-of-town at a Christian men's event. Holly's husband, John, was not a Christian, but he agreed to attend with Doyle. After all, what parent doesn't get excited at the thought of a weekend away from the kids? Knowing that the Christian event would express the love of Jesus to each man in attendance, Doyle and I were asking God for salvation to come to John and his family.

Near the end of an exhilarating day of rides and hotdogs, we sipped lemonade while sitting on a bench next to the classic roller coaster, The Racer. I stopped to call Doyle for a quick update on their trip. He shared continuously about all the marvelous things happening at the men's conference, hardly taking a breath. I'll never forget when he told me about Holly's husband John accepting Christ into his life. I looked up at the tall Racer and thought, "The news of John knowing Jesus is more exciting than this roller coaster and a fun day at a theme park." I was elated beyond words!

Holly, John and their family continued growing in the Lord and leading many to know Jesus. They started attending church, adopted children and pursued God's plan for their lives. Meeting God in one weekend changed the entire trajectory of their lives. The joy that filled our hearts was immeasurable.

SALVATION IS WAY BETTER THAN
KINGS ISLAND OR A POSITIVE
PREGNANCY TEST, AND THE GIFT OF
SALVATION IS EXTRA SWEET AS WE GET
TO EXPERIENCE THE JOY OF IT FOR
ETERNITY.

"Those the Lord has rescued will return. They will enter Zion with singing; everlasting joy will crown their heads. Gladness and joy will overtake them, and sorrow and sighing will flee away" (Isaiah 35:10).

The gospel brings joy, and sharing the gospel brings joy. Joy is found in reaching people for Jesus. It is one of the most significant investments you will ever make in your life, one that has lasting benefits not only on earth but also into eternity.

"Jesus instructed us: 'Therefore go and make disciples of all nations, baptizing them in the name of the Father and of the Son and the Holy Spirit'" (Matthew 28:19).

Often I am reminded of my "joy of salvation" on ordinary days in unexpected places. Recently, I was out of town visiting my sister's family, helping them prepare for my niece's high school graduation when God reminded me of the joy felt in sharing Jesus.

I relished all the last-minute details for Elle's celebration. Elle and I had a list of errands and exchanges to make in a short amount of time. First, zipping in and out of T.J. Maxx to look for a cute top we didn't find and then to Dollar Tree for photo frames. Check! Next, we arrived at Meijer for patio flowers, then on to McAllisters for a gigantic half-n-half iced tea, and finally, of course, to Hobby Lobby for cute baskets for her new dorm room. Lingering while looking at all the crafts, we spontaneously decided to buy birdhouses to paint together. They weren't on the list, but the unexpected idea gave us both an anticipatory smile. It was a girl's day that only an aunt can fully appreciate.

There she was, so grown up, graceful and intent on her new bright future and even more impressive that she was the one driving me around. We have much in common, such as a love for music that includes high school choir experience as alto ones. On this sunny June day, with iced teas in hand, we were happy. However, our happiness was not simply about the shopping and unexpected birdhouses. We were especially delighted because we shared the joy of salvation.

Getting into the car, she said to me, "I love driving with the windows rolled down." I said, "Me too." As we drove back to the house with the air in our hair, winding down roads of tree-lined streets encased with black-board fences and pastures of horses, we sang along with David Crowder on the radio. We belted out the lyrics at the top of our lungs, oblivious to musical perfection but well aware of God as our audience.

> "WHAT A FELLOWSHIP, WHAT A JOY DIVINE
> LEANING ON THE EVERLASTING ARMS
> WHAT A BLESSEDNESS, WHAT A PEACE IS MINE
> LEANING ON THE EVERLASTING ARMS
> LEANING, LEANING
> SAFE AND SECURE FROM ALL ALARMS
> LEANING, LEANING
> LEANING ON THE EVERLASTING ARMS."

My heart leaped knowing that we shared the thrill of unity in Him. These are the experiences that confirm God's presence. I submit there is no higher high on earth.

"Restore to me the joy of your salvation and grant me a willing spirit to sustain me" (Psalm 51:12).

Joy with Like-Minded
CHRISTIAN FRIENDS

"Her faithful people will ever sing for joy" (Psalm 132:16).

One of the highlights of my life happens once every month. Approximately a dozen friends from around our city of 2 million people gather together to pray. We appropriately named our group "Arise" as we arise to pray for our city and each other in the morning. One particular morning, we each carried an assortment of burdens. One friend had a severe marriage issue. One had an ill father in the hospital. One was the primary caregiver for two family members, and several were trying to manage job and career situations. Personally, I

MY HEART LEAPED KNOWING THAT WE SHARED THE THRILL OF UNITY IN HIM.

was sorting through my unreasonable fears of several upcoming deadlines. We mingled around the counter with fresh berries, yogurt and organic coffee, relaxing in the warm and casual atmosphere. Sharing about the trials we were facing, prayer popped up like popcorn around the room. It never ceases to amaze me how this varied group can almost instantaneously unite in prayer and faith.

"Be joyful in hope, patient in affliction, faithful in prayer" (Romans 12:12).

Someone finally corralled us to a circle for the true purpose of our gathering. We were there to worship God, pray for revival for our city, and naturally, we prayed for one another. So much heaviness was hanging in the air and the balance, so we started to sing. Travis led us with, "The joy of the Lord is our strength, He gives us living water, and we thirst no more... He fills our mouths with laughter...oh the joy of the Lord is my strength."

Spontaneous clapping broke out, and soon we were all in harmony rejoicing in the Lord. The energy was electric, and hope was there. Peace descended like a cloud. We began declaring the word of God, speaking out His goodness in praises and prayer. We covered everything He placed on our hearts, and we did that in anticipation and expectation of God hearing and answering us. We needed and strengthened one another.

"May the God of hope fill you with all joy and peace as you trust in Him so that you may overflow with hope by the power of the Holy Spirit" (Romans 15:13).

IT NEVER CEASES TO AMAZE ME HOW THIS VARIED GROUP CAN ALMOST INSTANTANEOUSLY UNITE IN PRAYER AND FAITH.

There is something significant about fully believing in prayer and faith with like-minded Christian friends while standing on the truth of God's Word. Find or start a group if you don't have one. It will bring you life, accountability, community and friendship.

"Then make my joy complete by being like-minded, having the same love, being one in spirit and of one mind" (Philippians 2:2).

Joy in Serving
AND REACHING OTHERS FOR JESUS

"And the disciples were filled with joy and with the Holy Spirit" (Acts 13:52).

Serving God in Kenya has taught me innumerable lessons. One particular lesson I learned by witnessing and receiving the servant-hearts of passionate faith leaders I encountered while there. One of the greatest gifts my Kenyan brothers and sisters offered to us was the gift of hospitality. I have never witnessed nor experienced anything like it. The leaders would physically run to bring us water to wash hands or drink. They would swoop in to carry our bags and Bibles and place them on our conference chairs. Grandmas cooked rice, greens and beans to serve the hundreds of guests. Their service was swift, intentional and full of joy. Though they had less than us materialistically, they helped and served with abundant grace, joy and generosity. It is a privilege to learn the pleasure of serving others from my brothers and sisters in Kenya.

THOUGH THEY HAD LESS THAN US MATERIALISTICALLY, THEY HELPED AND SERVED WITH ABUNDANT GRACE, JOY AND GENEROSITY.

Back home, it took me a while to realize the depth of opportunity to serve with such abundant grace and generosity was right in front of my nose in Columbus, Ohio. I returned from missions overseas with a newfound appreciation for street ministry. I had a new love for orphans, the sex-trafficked and sidelined people in my own backyard. So I could not wait to speak to a specific group of women within five miles of our home church. This particular meeting had paid security for the safety and well-being of those attending, and the theme was Princess Night. Girls and women ranging from age thirteen to seventy plus were in attendance.

Fresh showers and an opportunity to get a clean donated dress kicked off the afternoon. Shoes, jewelry and makeup finished the look. Generous women from our church helped prepare lasagna, salad, bread and dessert so that we could serve the guests of honor a delicious home-cooked meal. In addition, Princess Night had a red carpet runway, linen tables decorated with roses and scripture signs declaring, "He left the 99 for you" and "You are the pearl of great price." Music played as the women entered one by one. We celebrated them with cheers, claps and hugs as they made their way to our beautifully decorated dining hall. Eventually close to one hundred women filled our crowded space.

I stood speechless, looking around the room. Brokenness hovered in the atmosphere because each one had a story, and the stories included human trafficking, abuse and addiction. One newly single woman had her mouth wired shut and stitches all over her face from a severe punch. Another had heroin sores up and down both arms. Across the room, I glanced at a young woman I knew who had grown up at our church. We had helped her family for many years. I wondered if she recognized me. I thought to myself, "Maybe I can find her after the message." I hoped that she would still be there after the program.

Although I had a lesson prepared, I wondered what I could say to these women that would make a difference in their lives.

"Lord," I whispered, *"only you can bring a touch from heaven so powerful as to block out this darkness. Shine your light of joy and hope into their lives. Send your Holy Spirit to heal, deliver and care for each one. Amen."*

After several testimonies and songs, it was my turn. I stood up in shock at the hurt my soul felt. Empathy abounded from my heart for each situation. Then, mustering courage from the Lord, I started with, "Jesus has an encounter waiting for each one of you."

I then began to share the story of the woman at the well. I continued.

This story takes place in a tiny Israeli town called Shechem at a famous water well. All the great characters of the Bible had stopped there in times past. The Samaritan woman went to the well looking for water, but because of her dishonor, she went at a time when others would not be there. It was at this well where she had a life-changing encounter.

"Soon, a Samaritan woman came to draw water. Surprised, Jesus said to her, 'Give me a drink of water.', she said, 'Why would a Jewish man ask a Samaritan woman for a drink of water?' Jesus replied, 'If you only knew who I am and the gift that God wants to give you—you'd ask me for a drink, and I would give to you living water'" (John 4:8-10 TPT).

It's important to note that Jews and Samaritans were not supposed to associate with each other. How many of us have had similar thoughts as this Samaritan woman? I'm not good enough to associate with Jesus, or Jesus is too good for me. At first, she offered Jesus some pushback. She questioned and doubted Jesus, and she seemed almost defiant toward His offer of support.

"JESUS HAS AN ENCOUNTER WAITING FOR EACH ONE OF YOU."

"The woman replied, 'But sir, you don't even have a bucket, and this well is very deep. So, where do you find this 'living water'? Do you think that you are greater than our ancestor Jacob who dug this well and drank from it himself, along with his children and livestock?'" (John 4:11-12 TPT).

Jesus did not give up. Instead, he graciously extended His offer again, and despite her pushback, she ultimately could not refuse Jesus.

"Jesus answered, 'If you drink from Jacob's well, you'll be thirsty again and again, but if anyone drinks the living water I give them, they will never thirst again and will be forever satisfied! For when you drink the water, I give you, it becomes a gushing fountain of the Holy Spirit, springing up and flooding you with endless life!' So the woman replied, 'Let me drink that water so I'll never be thirsty again and won't have to come back here to draw water'" (John 4:11-15 TPT).

The lessons from this passage are many, and I want to highlight a few:

For whatever reason, the Samaritan woman went for water, isolated and alone. Sometimes the best appointments of our life are during times alone, one on one with Jesus. She met Him by herself that afternoon. He casually and lovingly looked at her and said more than "How are you?" He extended a message that said, "You are valuable and I care. I love you. Tell me what you want. Tell me what you need." He does the same for us.

"TELL ME WHAT YOU WANT. TELL ME WHAT YOU NEED."

We all must encounter Jesus one by one, face to face. He longs to share with us and to look at us in love and anticipation. We never feel ready for this conversation.

Why me? I'm not acceptable, or my past is too messed up. I'm not worthy. We are always surprised, just like the woman at the well was.

God provided a well for this woman, and there is a well waiting for you. There is a deep well of hope for your future dreams. Jesus is the well of fresh, living water that never runs dry.

One of the fascinating things about Jesus in this story is that He was weary. God in heaven decided that He should send His Son to earth so that He could physically understand our struggles and feel the thirst and weariness of our souls. Jesus, fully divine, experienced life as fully human. In his humanity, He kindly and gently asked the woman, "Can you give me a drink?" He tore down barriers of sex, race, religion and position in that moment.

In a short time, Jesus offered her more than all the previous men in her life. He offered her water that wells up for eternity. I can imagine that she said, "Give me this water, so I'm not thirsty again. I'm tired of being tired all the time. I'm tired of being thirsty all the time. I need refreshment, and I need your cool living water."

The story does not stop there. God had even more in store for her, and He has even more in store for us.

"Jesus said, 'Go get your husband and bring him back here.' 'But I'm not married,' the woman answered. 'That's true,' Jesus said, 'for you've been married five times, and now you're living with a man who is not your husband. You have told the truth.' The woman said, 'You must be a prophet!'" (John 4:16-24 TPT).

Wow! Check it out! We see that He chose her. He knew

everything about her past, and He chose her anyway. He chose her because He loved her unconditionally. He knew her deepest and darkest secrets, her past and her pain. He saw her, and He loved her. He didn't scold her or shame her. He simply met her right where she was, and He loved her.

HE KNEW EVERYTHING ABOUT HER PAST AND HE CHOSE HER ANYWAY.

He does the same for us. He knows you, your story and your past, and He chooses you despite your mess. He doesn't show up in our lives to criticize us. Rather He meets us right where we are, and He loves us.

In this moment, the woman tries to wrap her mind around this love encounter and conversation with this man.

"The woman said, 'This is all so confusing, but I do know that the Anointed One is coming—the true Messiah. And when he comes, he will tell us everything we need to know.' Jesus said to her, 'You don't have to wait any longer, the Anointed One is here speaking with you—I am the One you're looking for'" (John 4:25-34 TPT).

She was astounded at the truth of meeting and knowing Jesus. She ran with great joy to share her news. Now that her shame was lifted, she didn't keep this good news to herself. Her new story begins. When God meets us and transforms us, we get to share that good news with others so that they too can know God's transformative love.

"So there were many from the Samaritan village who became believers in Jesus because of the woman's testimony: 'He told me everything I ever did!' Then they begged Jesus to stay with them, so he stayed there for two days, resulting in many more coming to faith in him because of his teachings. Then the Samaritans said to the woman, 'We no longer believe just because of what you told us, but now we've heard him ourselves and are convinced that he really is the true Savior of the world!'" (John 4:39-42 TPT).

Her new purpose began! She learned and grew in knowledge and understanding with Jesus. He transformed her from a woman who hid from the world to a joy-filled leader with a role of courage, freedom and influence. You can sense her fresh joy as she drinks in this holy living water. She could worship now with her entire heart because of the Holy Spirit who knew her story.

SHE COULD WORSHIP NOW WITH HER ENTIRE HEART BECAUSE OF THE HOLY SPIRIT WHO KNEW HER STORY.

Tell me, is this your moment? Are you sitting by the well? Drink deep wherever you are. You are not alone. Your pain is valid, and God sees you. I want you to ask Him for what you need. Ask Jesus to do for you, emotionally and physically, just as He did for the woman at the well. Welcome Him into your heart, and connect your heart to His tonight. He is here. He sees, and He knows. You are chosen. We have all been women at the well. Come and drink deep.

When I finished speaking, I watched as the women stood up, many holding hands, some in tears, and together, as a body of women desperate for Jesus, we prayed:

Dear Jesus,
You are the first person in my life to pay attention to me and notice the details. You know my past has weighed heavy on my shoulders. I ask you to rescue me. I need you. I admit, my life has been dry, and my heart hardened. Even though I find it difficult to imagine progress, I welcome you into my soul to soften me. Rush in and save me. You know everything I've ever done, and you still love me. The relationships in my life have messed up my

ability to trust or see clearly. Will you heal my mind and emotional wounds? I'm tired of looking back, and some things need to be forgotten forever. I run forward knowing that you will take care of this. I desperately want freedom.

Jesus, you are the best news I've had in a long time. Oh, thank you! How can I say it enough? You are good. I can't wait to share this hope with the people in my life that I love the most. I'm sure they will love you too after seeing the new me! Come closer now, and refresh me with Your pure living water. Let this water fall on me like spring rain. Wash away the shame, the guilt and the pain. Your well is deep. I feel it restoring my spirit, breathing new life into my lungs and cleansing me. For once in my life, I belong, I belong to You. Jesus, we are a perfect match! Amen.

After the prayer, I stood overlooking a crowd of some of the most courageous women I have ever known. Following my story about the woman at the well, our team eagerly handed out tote bags full of gifts, including much-needed toiletries. It felt like a birthday party. I spotted the young lady who grew up at our church and went immediately toward her. She remembered me. We hugged for a long time. She was full of hope, having been reminded of God's love for her and the value He placed on her precious life.

Rejoicing in Finding Lost Treasure

The woman at the well was lost, and many of the women at Princess Night were lost. They had yet to encounter Jesus. Maybe your son or daughter is lost. Perhaps you are lost. Jesus cares deeply for lost people, and so should we. He urges us in three similar illustrations to see the importance of seeking "hidden things," and He parallels "joy" as the reward we will receive. In these parables, He talks about treasure, coins and sheep. All three are precious. He wants us to see the value in searching for the misplaced. Who do you love that is nowhere to be found? Are you searching for them? Is Jesus searching for you?

"The kingdom of heaven is like treasure hidden in a field. When a man found it, he hid it again, and then in his joy went and sold all he had and bought that field" (Matthew 13:44).

"Or suppose a woman has ten silver coins and loses one. Doesn't she light a lamp, sweep the house and search carefully until she finds it? And when she finds it, she calls her friends and neighbors together and says, 'Rejoice with me; I have found my lost coin'" (Luke 15:8-9).

"Suppose one of you has a hundred sheep and loses one of them. Doesn't he leave the ninety-nine in the open country and go after the lost sheep until he finds it? And when he finds it, he joyfully puts it on his shoulders and goes home. Then he calls his friends and neighbors together and says, 'Rejoice with me; I have found my lost sheep'" (Luke 15:4-6).

It's hard to imagine how God feels when one of his lost children returns home. I know the joy of finding something lost, but that is only a fraction of what God feels when one of his children return to Him.

When we lived in the country, I had a toy poodle Graham (yes, I named him after Billy Graham). He was an eight pound farm dog. We lived on six acres, and Graham would bolt like lightning out the back door and run like the wind. Because he ran at super speed, I spent many hours of my life chasing and looking for him. Usually, he was found somewhere on the property, but one day he was lost - really lost. I panicked because I was late for work, but I just couldn't leave him outside. I walked for an hour, looking for him in all the usual places and calling his name. Nothing. Then I got in the car and drove for a lengthy hour, calling his name out the window while scouring the fields for any trace of him. Again, nothing.

I finally returned home. I was defeated and imagined the worst. Though I was beyond late for work, I sat down next to the kitchen window, feeling sad and entirely out of sorts. Debating on what to do next, something small and red caught the corner of my eye. From outside the window, I saw my tiny poodle racing toward me. Covered in briars, sticks and a few cuts, little Graham was racing back to the house. He was home! I was so happy to have found him that all my frustration melted away into snuggles.

The joy I felt that day is merely a fraction of what God experiences when His children return to Him. Consider your most coveted possession or loved one. Now imagine them lost only to one day be found again. Can you picture the joy? Now consider that you are the one who is lost, and your heavenly Father is desperately seeking after you. The heavens erupt in happiness when God's children return home to Him. Can you sense the joy? Can you imagine the party of rejoicing?

REFLECT
choose one or two questions

Whether on your own or in a community of others, ask these questions and apply them to your life.

- Do you like the windows down in your car or house? Or do you prefer air conditioning?

- What is your favorite theme park? Do you like to ride roller coasters, play games or go to shows?

- Do you like to drink water? Share your drink of choice? Tea, coffee or something else?

- What is your style? Casual, dressy or somewhere in between?

PRAY
this sentence prayer aloud as a group

Dear God,
Renew my joy of salvation, and open my eyes to see those who need to know You. Help me to share my excitement about You with others.
Amen.

READ
take turns reading aloud

JOHN 4:8-10 TPT
Soon a Samaritan woman came to draw water. Surprised, Jesus said to her, "Give me a drink of water", she said, "Why would a Jewish man ask a Samaritan woman for a drink of water?" Jesus replied, "If you only knew who I am and the gift that God wants to give you—you'd ask me for a drink, and I would give to you living water."

JOHN 4:11-15 TPT
Jesus answered, "If you drink from Jacob's well, you'll be thirsty again and again, but if anyone drinks the living water I give them, they will never thirst again and will be forever satisfied! For when you drink the water I give you, it becomes a gushing fountain of the Holy Spirit, springing up and flooding you with endless life!" The woman replied, "Let me drink that water so I'll never be thirsty again and won't have to come back here to draw water."

JOHN 4:39-42 TPT
So there were many from the Samaritan village who became believers in Jesus because of the woman's testimony: "He told me everything I ever did!" Then they begged Jesus to stay with them, so he stayed there for two days, resulting in many more coming to faith in him because of his teachings. Then the Samaritans said to the woman, "We no longer believe just because of what you told us, but now we've heard him ourselves and are convinced that he really is the true Savior of the world!"

MATTHEW 13:44
The kingdom of heaven is like treasure hidden in a field. When a man found it, he hid it again, and then in his joy went and sold all he had and bought that field.

CONNECTION
Answer these questions together

In Psalm 51:12, King David says, "Restore to me the joy of your salvation and grant me a willing spirit to sustain me." What does this mean to you? Jennifer talks about experiencing "the joy of salvation" with a friend at Kings Island and her niece. Do either of these stories resonate with you? How have you renewed your faith?

In John 4:11-15, Jesus talks about living water. What does He mean? How has knowing Jesus refreshed your life like a drink of water?

Does anything about this story surprise or stand out to you?
What about:
How Jesus talked to her despite the cultural divide?
His insight into her personal life?
How she shared this new hope with the entire town?

Jesus extended grace and salvation to the woman at the well. How has Jesus shown up for you in a loving way?

In Matthew 13:44, Jesus talks about the pearl of great price. "The kingdom of heaven is like treasure hidden in a field. When a man found it, he hid it again, and then in his joy went and sold all he had and bought that field."
Who do you know that you are ready to share the love of Jesus? What lengths are you willing to go to find lost treasure and share Jesus with them? Why do you think this can be difficult?

Are you a prodigal? Did you stray from God but finally come home? Share your story.

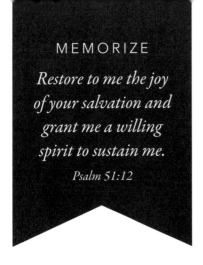

PRAYER POINTS

Ask God to restore your joy about salvation and refresh your faith.

Specifically, call aloud the names of people in your life who need to know Jesus.

GROUP CHALLENGE

Practice sharing your testimony with your group

Share your testimony with at least one person this week. Invite them to pray with you or to accept Jesus. Next week share with your group what happened.

Share your story on the Simply for Women radio show with Jennifer. Come together!

GROUP ACTIVITY

Go on an outing together with an outreach ministry that fights human trafficking.

Serve a meal at a food kitchen, and talk to the women there who need God's love.

Journal
AT HOME

Write a prayer to Jesus as your first love. Share honestly about any place in your life that has lost the joy of salvation. Ask Him to restore this love and happiness.

Make a list of lost people who need to know the Lord. Pray for them to "come home" to Jesus. Then pray for them individually by name.

Journal
AT HOME

Pray this prayer and expand on any portion that speaks to you.

Dear Jesus,

You are the first person in my life to pay attention to me and notice the details. You know my past has weighed heavy on my shoulders. I ask you to rescue me. I need you. I admit, my life has been dry, and my heart hardened. Even though I find it difficult to imagine progress, I welcome you into my soul to soften me. Rush in and save me. You know everything I've ever done, and you still love me. The relationships in my life have messed up my ability to trust or see clearly. Will you heal my mind and emotional wounds? I'm tired of looking back, and some things need to be forgotten forever. I run forward knowing that you will take care of this. I desperately want freedom.

Jesus, you are the best news I've had in a long time. Oh, thank you! How can I say it enough? You are good. I can't wait to share this hope with the people in my life that I love the most. I'm sure they will love you too after seeing the new me! Come closer now, and refresh me with Your pure living water. Let this water fall on me like spring rain. Wash away the shame, the guilt and the pain. Your well is deep. I feel it restoring my spirit, breathing new life into my lungs and cleansing me. For once in my life, I belong, I belong to You. Jesus, we are a perfect match! Amen.

KALE SALAD

INGREDIENTS

Salad

Large bunch of fresh kale, *washed and chopped in small pieces*

1 ½ cups of cooked and cooled quinoa

Pine nuts *(you can use English walnuts to save expense)*

Feta cheese *(one container)*

Dried cranberries *(at least one cup)*

Dressing

Juice of two or three fresh lemons

Olive oil

Salt

Fresh Thyme *(I use an entire container because I love the taste, this makes the salad)*

DIRECTIONS

Mix all the ingredients together in a big tupperware with lid because this salad is great leftover the next day and you can shake it up this way as well. Add as much of the dressing ingredients as you like to taste.

This recipe is from my dear friend Teresa Smith.

CHAPTER

5

Joy Keepers and Joy Stealers

When it comes to true joy, here is what we covered so far:

> Joy prevails no matter the external circumstances (unlike happiness that comes and goes like the tide.)
>
> Jesus is the source of true, everlasting joy because He is true, everlasting joy.
>
> Joy is available to us when we commit our hearts to Jesus.
>
> Joy is a fruit of the Spirit that we must cultivate in our lives.
>
> The path to experiencing joy begins with Jesus and is cultivated by spending time with Him, His word and His people.
>
> There is no greater joy than in the presence of Jesus.
>
> Joy is found in our relationships when Jesus is at the center.
>
> Sharing Jesus with others is the best way to spread joy.

Don't these truths make you want to run to Jesus? Knowing that He promises unending joy motivates me to seek more of Him. Happiness is good, but Jesus didn't promise us happiness. In fact, He warned that we would have troubles. There will always be dark, harsh and evil things around us because we live in a fallen world, but joy can still be present in us because of Christ.

The major league win is that once we have developed joy as a fruit in our lives, it is difficult to lose joy even in hard times. However, our experience of joy does ebb and flow with our level of maturity in Christ. Here's the stabilizing secret - grow in Jesus and you will grow in joy!

Choose Joy

In addition to cultivating joy in our lives, there is one simple step we can take to have more joy, and it is this: Choose joy.

I know it seems obvious or maybe even cliche, but choosing joy can be a game changer in your life.

When my niece Anna was little, she would hum in the highchair with happiness whenever she knew she was going to eat carbs. She loved bread or dough of any kind, as we all do, right? My sister and I thought this was hilarious. Carbs became a joke between us since she and I seem to live on a perpetual diet. When we order pizza, we start humming "hmm, hmm, hmm," just like little Anna would whenever we set bread down on her tray.

That simple hum from my tiny niece was an act of joy that spread into my life and my sister's life. After all, happiness is contagious. While Anna spreads joy without trying, you and I have the opportunity to hand out joy intentionally.

Are you willing to be a joy super spreader? Once you determine to choose joy for your own life, you can quickly spread it to the lives of others. Spreading joy is as simple as offering a note of encouragement, a happy smile or a warm hug.

ARE YOU WILLING TO BE A JOY SUPER SPREADER?

One afternoon, Doyle and I met with some leaders at church to have them pray with us about my upcoming mastectomy surgery. I honestly dreaded this meeting because sharing the news was hard. After the leaders offered many sweet-filled prayers, I stood alone in the lobby while everyone mingled around. I was emotionally exhausted and ready to go home. Suddenly one of my favorite leaders wrapped me in the biggest bear hug, permeating my heart. That unexpected kindness softened my exhaustion and bolstered my heart, like a jolt of joy energy to lift my spirit. Joy does that. It fills the mind, energizes the spirit and then overflows to minister hope to those around you.

Humming over thick-cut pizza and offering an unexpected hug aren't the only ways to express joy. Joy is expressed in a myriad of ways. The point isn't how you express and share joy. The point is that you do it however it comes naturally to you. Maybe you aren't a hugger but you have a memorable laugh. Maybe you find joy in dancing, singing or encouraging others. Maybe joy in your life is evident as you find what makes you come alive and you pursue whatever that is. No matter how you express and share joy, the point is - just do it!

To this day, I can close my eyes and see Granny Hazel's kitchen as if I was standing there right now. She lived in a white farmhouse, and although it was old and imperfect, it did not matter because she was there. I can still hear the porch door clink behind me as I hurried past the sunroom and into Granny's arms. Her welcoming embrace was animated and passionate with "Granny Hazel kisses" overflowing on my cheeks. Looking back, I am fascinated by her consistency. She never failed to express delight to her grandkids when we arrived. Simply the thought of her memory fills my spirit with joy.

I want to be like that, don't you? What if guests in your home sensed joy and refreshment in your presence whenever they visited you? What if joy was an atmosphere of wonder and delight, humor and fun, charm and comfort in your home? When joy is found, you must not keep it inside; instead, share it with everyone you meet.

It's easy to choose and spread joy when life is seemingly easy, but what about choosing joy when life is brutally hard?

I was amazed by a dear one from church who lost her husband unexpectedly a year and a half ago. I was there at the hospital that horrible night when he passed. The shock and grief were unbearable. On the day of their anniversary, she and I chatted over the phone. She said she knew he would want her to celebrate her life and move forward in joy. She added that her network of women from church had been a gift of strength during this challenging time in her life, and her new grandbaby filled her with such joy. Though her grief brought with it many dark days, my friend remained devoted to God, her faith and friends. I could see that she was an overcomer. Though experiencing deep pain and loss, she had a solid foundation in Jesus, and she still had joy.

While some of us are experiencing something as tragic as the loss of a loved one, most of us are experiencing the day-in and day-out difficulties that are a part of life. Too often, we are mentally defeated or overwhelmed. Just like one can feel heavy and bloated after overeating, our minds can feel weighed down by our excessive thoughts and feelings. We all deal with constant pressures. Many are self-induced. Others are an unavoidable part of life. Are you dealing with a mountain of daily tasks, bills, errands and work that never seem to end? In addition to our daily burdens, we carry a heaping stress pile that includes our physical health, relationship maintenance, financial worries and questions about our future. Something as simple as the rising price of gas can easily throw us over the edge.

WE ALL DEAL WITH CONSTANT PRESSURES.

We are a society of people living in a state of chronic stress so it is no wonder that joy seems to be fleeting! Thankfully Jesus is not. He is always with us, and when we maintain an ongoing connection with Him, we maintain a connection with the source of true, everlasting joy. By remembering that you always have access to joy via the Holy Spirit, you can boldly ask for and enter into joy no matter the situation around you.

No matter if you are facing your deepest loss or the everyday hardships of life this side of heaven, remember this: joy really is possible no matter how dark, low or desolate the circumstances that surround you.

In choosing joy, it is important to remember that joy is yours to keep. Consider it like a treasured piece of jewelry that you fasten around your wrist or fit snugly around your finger.

So I think this begs the question. How do we keep joy, and how do we lose it?

Throughout the rest of this chapter, I will provide suggestions for how you can keep the joy of the Lord, and then I'm going to suggest ways in which you might be tempted to lose joy. Remember, joy is yours to keep. Choose joy and keep it. I hope that these joy-keeping suggestions and joy-stealing warnings help you to move the fog out of the way and enter into a place where you can walk out your days with abundant joy.

Keeping and Losing Joy
THROUGH THE WORDS WE SPEAK

A powerful way to keep joy comes through our mouths. In other words, what we speak out loud can impact the solace we experience in our hearts. Even more simply put, let out a shout! "Praise the Lord," "Thank you, God," or "I trust you, Lord!" Once these words are expressed, the air we breathe seems to change. As the Psalmist teaches, try to verbally express shouts of praise throughout your day and see how it helps you keep joy. Joy is released through your mouth in a free voice. Why is opening it so hard? That is my challenge to you right now. Stop reading for a minute and give a shout of praise. Try it! Speaking aloud breaks through your pain, silence and fear.

"Then my head will be exalted above the enemies who surround me; at his sacred tent, I will sacrifice with shouts of joy; I will sing and make music to the Lord" (Psalm 27:6).

"SING HIM A NEW SONG; PLAY
SKILLFULLY, AND SHOUT FOR JOY."
Psalm 33:3

While praising God through our words can manifest joy, doubting God's presence in your life through your words can threaten your daily satisfaction. Consider these two examples. Which one do you think fosters joy, and which one is likely to steal joy?

"God, I need You. I praise You. You are my provider. You have never failed me. I know You will come through. You always do."

or

"I'm so bummed. Nothing is working out the way I thought it would. I don't know who I can trust. I guess I can only trust myself."

We can easily find ways to complain. Have you tried the discipline of keeping your mouth shut when something negative is happening? Silence instead of fussing is like exercise, hard at the moment but gratifying later. On the other hand, once it flies out of our mouths, grumbling will invariably destroy our joy.

The Israelites were known for this. Again and again, the Israelites complained and grumbled. They wanted better food and better water. Moses continually went before the Lord on their behalf, and God would answer him. God sent them fresh manna every day, and

God sent quail, but then they complained about the manna and the quail. Ultimately God's best for our lives is to live with gratitude even in harsh situations and thank Him at all times to keep our joy.

"DO EVERYTHING WITHOUT GRUMBLING OR ARGUING."
Philippians 2:14

In the same way that speaking negatively or complaining can make us feel "down," positive words can "lift" us up when speaking life-giving phrases.

Another way the words we speak can help us keep or lose joy is in asking God for forgiveness. When we open our mouths to confess any wrongdoing, it brings freedom and happiness. On the other hand, when we keep our sins a secret, joy is quenched.

1 John 1:9 says if we confess our sins He is faithful and just to forgive us.

Keep your joy through the uplifting words you speak, and allow your mouth to be a defender of your joy rather than a place that threatens to steal your joy or someone else's.

KEEP JOY WITH WORDS	LOSE JOY WITH WORDS
WORDS OF THE BIBLE	WORDS OF DOUBTING
WORDS OF POSITIVITY	WORDS OF COMPLAINING
WORDS OF PRAISE TO GOD	WORDS OF CRITICIZING
WORDS OF CONFESSION	WORDS OF SECRECY

Choosing a God-is-in-control attitude

MAINTAINS JOY WHILE LIVING STRESSED STEALS GLADNESS

Traveling back and forth overseas to Kenya and Israel, I learned to relax, especially when leading a team. While traveling between 24-30 hours, stress is inevitable. Flights are delayed and even canceled. Teams get tired, cranky and hangry. Sleep is limited. Sometimes the travel is such that we miss a meal or find ourselves trying to sleep on an airport floor with our backpack as a pillow. Inconveniences or frustrations are part of life and part of traveling. Determination to travel relaxed or tense can make the difference between keeping joy or allowing it to be stolen.

Do you ever have days or even weeks that just don't go as planned? Last week a friend canceled our dinner reservations at the last minute because she had to work late. I understood but had been looking forward to this treat all week. Disappointment crept in and threatened to steal my joy. It was up to me to put on gladness and accept what I could not change.

One of my favorite mentors is Corrie ten Boom. I remember when she wrote about being in a concentration camp with her sister Betsy during World War II. Their bunk room had fleas in the bed. Corrie complained, and Betsy encouraged her to thank God for the fleas. Corrie did. Because of the fleas, the prison guards refused to come into the room. As a result, Corrie and her sister could lead Bible studies for all the girls at night. This story still inspires me.

"Lord, I trust you today" is a simple prayer that I pray often. I have discovered that the root of my discouragement is generally that I need to humble myself and admit a lack of trust in God. Saying, "I trust You," is a way to acknowledge Him at every slow moment in the day when you have a bit of time to give God your trust, even in seemingly small situations that we don't understand. There is soothing joy in trusting. We don't have all of our questions answered, but we trust the Lord. We can't see the future, but we trust the Lord. We can't control the decisions or actions of others, but we trust the Lord. My heart is hurting because of the evil we see, but we trust the Lord.

"Bring joy to your servant, Lord, for I put my trust in you" (Psalm 86:4).

Obedience Leads to Joy
AND DISOBEDIENCE LEADS TO JOY LOST

Have you ever played a matching word game? If the word was obedience, what might come to your mind first? Probably something like "rules" or "restrictions." My guess is one word you would not use is "joy." Joy and obedience don't seem to fit together. Joy seems liberating; obedience sounds restrictive. Joy conveys lightheartedness; obedience seems burdensome. Most of us would never think that the way to true joy in life lies on the path of obedience to God, but it does!

For decades I have been serving on pastoral staff in the local church, and it continues to be the greatest privilege of my life. As a result of my years in ministry, I have met some of the most phenomenal people. One thing most of them have in common is this: they are wonderfully obedient. They honor God at home and church. Their lives may not be exciting (by the world's definition), but they are steady, consistent and dependable. Cheerful believers come week in and week out to the house of God. They serve Him gladly in various roles, encouraging the younger ones coming up in the faith. Their tithes are practical. Their prayers are frequent. They generously give their hard-earned dollars to see the work of God continue for the church, building repairs, feeding the poor or sharing the gospel through media and outreach. They are consistently seen with hands raised to God in praise in the sanctuary. I am pleased to witness this community of saints. I marvel at their reverence for Him and the fruit of joy that sustains them.

Happiness shines through their lives because they obey God. Obedience is a pattern for them. Through one-on-one discipleship, these obedient saints mentor others, love their community and reach the lost. They are dependable both inside and outside the church walls, and it is truly a joy to call these faithful ones my church family.

JOY COMES WHEN YOU RESPOND TO A
HOLY GOD IN FAITHFUL OBEDIENCE.

"And her faithful people will ever sing for joy" (Psalm 132:16).

"...all you need to say is a simple 'Yes' or 'No'" (James 5:12).

In 2 Chronicles 30:1-27, King Hezekiah's story reveals he was a godly king who resolved to restore personal and national worship as the top priority in the first year of his reign. He cleansed and restored the temple. He reinstituted the sacrifices. Hezekiah invited the whole nation to observe the Passover in Jerusalem. The result was the most remarkable worship celebration since the division of the kingdom.

The theme of heartfelt, joyful obedience repeatedly occurs throughout the chapter, as Judah and many others in Israel join together to celebrate the Passover. "The hand of God was also on Judah to give them one heart to do what the king and princes commanded by the word of the Lord." The mood of the conference was "great joy." They had such a good time that they decided to keep going for an extra week! They didn't want it to end. Though some mocked and refused to come, those who obeyed found the deep and lasting joy only God can give.

"The whole assembly then agreed to celebrate the festival seven more days, so for another seven days, they celebrated joyfully" (2 Chronicles 30:21-23).

Do you notice what it says? It says, "the whole assembly then agreed." In other words, they collectively chose to celebrate. They CHOSE joy. Our obedience can look like choosing to celebrate and choosing positivity. Don't you love that? Sometimes obedience is a discipline of doing things that we don't want to do, and other times obedience is simply choosing positivity, a smile, a cheery disposition, a celebration, encouragement or laughter. Sometimes we just need to put on joy and see what happens when we do. It's kind of like "fake it till you make it." I'm not suggesting that you cover up your pain with a disingenuous smile. Rather I'm suggesting that there are times when we simply need to choose joy or **choose to go to church**. You might be surprised by what transpires in your heart when you do.

When we surrender our lives to God's ways and not our own, we begin to mature and enjoy all that God has for us through obedience. Similarly, disobedience is a guaranteed way to lose the joy of the Lord. As a result, we watch our joy slip away.

Surrender and obedience work together to bring joy, whereas our stubbornness and our disobedience work together to keep us from experiencing God's fullness, including joy. Commit yourself to obedience, and discover the joy that comes from living aligned with God's best for you.

Admitting weakness to God
IS A WAY TO KEEP JOY WHILE CONTROLLING PEOPLE OR THINGS WILL STEAL OUR JOY

Have you ever considered that God has allowed weakness in your life so that you might experience more joy in Him? It seems contradictory, but think about it. When we acknowledge our lack and acknowledge God's power, we create space in our life to enJOY more of who God is to us.

Paul understood this very well. He even had a physical imperfection of some sort that he said was to keep him from becoming conceited. Our shortcomings and the weaknesses of those we love have the potential to keep us from walking in humility and relying on God's strength. When we want everything physically, relationally and practically to always go as planned, then we lose our joy. Taking delight in our weaknesses may seem like a contradiction, but it keeps us on our knees and seeking the Lord for answers.

"Or because of these surpassingly great revelations. Therefore, to keep me from becoming conceited, I was given a thorn in my flesh, a messenger of Satan, to torment me. Three times I pleaded with the Lord to take it away from me.

"But he said to me, 'My grace is sufficient for you, for my power is made perfect in weakness.' Therefore I will boast more gladly about my weaknesses so that Christ's power may rest on me. That is why, for Christ's sake, I delight in weaknesses, in insults, in hardships, in persecutions, in difficulties. For when I am weak, then I am strong" (2 Corinthians 12:7-10).

What about control? I know someone who has to have everything perfect all the time. She keeps a spotless house, a clutter-free car, beautifully coiffed hair and up-to-date framed family photos in her decorated home. Don't get me wrong. I enjoy it when my house is clean, especially when the laundry is fresh and neatly put away. A tidy home is not the problem. The problem is controlling "things" or people. The dilemma is when we have to have everything our way, a certain way, all of the time.

Control strips us of joy. Sometimes people say things they don't mean or do things they shouldn't do, and we have to let it go. Their pessimistic ways will quench our happiness and steal our joy. If we aren't careful, we can quickly lose our joy over the little things. Trying by yourself to keep everything or everyone going in one direction can cause anxiety. Take it to the Lord, take a deep breath and let it go.

"When anxiety was great within me, your consolation brought me joy" (Psalm 94:19).

Staying in His company fosters joy
WHILE DISTRACTIONS STEAL OUR JOY.

We discussed this at length in Chapter 2, but it is such a critical component to our experience of joy that I must mention it again. The fastest way to experience joy is in the presence of Jesus.

My room in Kenya was on the second floor. Exhausted after a full day of ministering to women, I arrived at my room late in the evening. I was fully expecting to fall into bed and fast asleep, but surprisingly, my eyes were wide awake. I heard every bug chirp, listened to cows "moo" in the distance and sensed the security guard checking the grounds. "Lord, please, I just want to sleep and be prepared for another big day tomorrow." Tossing, turning and praying, I was still awake with eyes that seemed to be opening even more.

Reluctantly caving into what I assumed was God's prompting, I got out my Bible and journal and began to write notes about the great hand of God that I had witnessed in our meetings that day. Still wide awake, I got out of bed, flipped on the light switch and quickly remembered that the electricity was suspended for four hours each night. Deciding again to stop fighting the sleep that simply would not come, I chose to sing in the dark.

Listening to worship music on my phone, I began to pray for the women I had met. I prayed for the leaders, the upcoming gatherings, the medical clinic, the orphans and the widows. I prayed for healing and miracles, salvations and deliverances. I started to catch a glimpse of His heart for these people. As the sun began to rise, I felt His loving touch for humanity.

Sometimes it takes spending our most precious commodity and currency - time - to receive the fullness of His presence. When the Lord is absent, joy is gone. Distractions are everywhere, and distractions can easily take over and keep us from Him. Absence is a joy destroyer. Whatever it takes to re-enter his company, whatever we have to do to get back in his presence, it is worth it every time.

Many times I have drifted away from Jesus. It is easy to do. Usually it is when I decide to wake up and immediately jump on the computer to check my email, pull out the calendar, rearrange meetings and tasks, and add more to-do lists. There is nothing inherently wrong with my approach, but before I know it, I have spent the entire day into the night busy at work. I seem to slide by for a day or two with no problems, but I feel the anxiety rise after several days. Generally, I fall exhausted into my Father's lap and say, "Ok, I give. I did it again. Forgive me. I tried to go on my strength, thinking I could afford the luxury of a few days or a week on my own. I was wrong and I need you, Lord."

Don't get me wrong, there is grace for the hectic seasons, but completely ignoring God is what I'm talking about. The best and most fulfilling way to journey through life is to submit your time to God throughout your day. I love including God in the mundane and talking to Him about everything. Here is a short prayer I started years ago to get me back on track.

> Dear God,
> I want to want you more. I long to long for you. Increase my desire. Draw me with your Holy Spirit.
> > Amen

"You make known to me the path of life; you will fill me with joy in your presence, with eternal pleasures at your right hand" (Psalm 16:11).

"To him who is able to keep you from stumbling and to present you before his glorious presence without fault and with great joy" (Jude 1:24).

Celebrating others brings joy,
WHILE JEALOUSY IS SURE TO STEAL IT

When was the last time you celebrated on behalf of a friend? When we rejoice over the successes of others, we receive collective joy. For example, we have a dear friend Phil Joel in a world-famous band, the NewsBoys. Recently, they held a successful year of re-union tours. We were so excited! Phil, Doyle and I sat outdoors on a restaurant patio for hours and recounted the goodness of God and His answers to our prayers. It brought us such joy to celebrate the joy in Phil's life.

Joining others in celebrating what God is doing in their lives helps us to experience God's heart of joy. On the flipside, when we envy what our friend, neighbor or stranger has, we rob God of the opportunity to gift us joy through all of the good and grace He has placed in our own lives.

Here is a helpful definition of jealousy: thinking God doesn't have "enough" for your life, physically or spiritually. Believing He only has enough for the lives of other people.

I know a woman who sincerely wanted what her friends had. Brianne had a circle of friends who had boats, several children and disposable income. She wanted all of this too. My friend's husband worked hard, and they had an attractive home with more than enough for the two of them, yet she was discontent. Marriage stress followed because her husband had no way to physically have kids or earn a living at the level of the others, and Brianne wouldn't stop pushing for more.

Coveting what a friend has can be so damaging that you lose all pleasure in what you do have, even losing joy with the people God has placed in your circle of friends. Envy happens when you don't trust God to meet your needs and fail to believe that He is more than enough for you. When we start to look around and compare ourselves to others, we lose sight of God's specific provision for us. We all have friends with more time, resources, emotional strength or even fulfillment through family relations. When we focus on what they have and look at what we lack, we lose our joy.

Allow the rise of jealousy in your spirit to be a red flag that alerts you to a slippery slope ahead. Just like blind spot detectors tell you to stay in your lane, the feeling of jealousy tells us that we are on track to destruction if we keep veering in that direction. Instead, be someone who celebrates the successes of others and encourages your sisters and brothers.

Be a celebrator, and watch the joy flow.

WHEN WE START TO LOOK AROUND AND COMPARE OURSELVES TO OTHERS, WE LOSE SIGHT OF GOD'S SPECIFIC PROVISION FOR US.

Fighting steals joy
WHILE SURRENDER INVITES JOY INTO OUR LIVES

Surrendering to God promotes peace and joy in our lives. Remember, God is on your side. He is fighting for you despite what you can or cannot see, think or feel. His ways are not your ways, and His perfect plan is for your good. He is for you. Surrender to Him and let the joy surround you.

While surrender promotes joy and peace, fighting leads to a swift lack of joy.

One day at the church office, a couple came in to talk to us about their marriage. We met in my husband's office, which has lightweight sliding doors. Many staff worked quietly at their desks down the hallway while we sat behind a closed door, hoping to encourage this couple. Within five minutes of our meeting, they erupted in a screaming match. Soon we realized there wasn't much that we had to offer. No amount of coercion or calming could get them to stop fighting. I'm not even sure that they wanted a referee.

Finally, after about fifteen minutes, one of the staffers opened the doors and stuck their head in to check on us, "Are you all ok in here?" "Yes, and we are just now finished," I replied. I took my cue to walk the couple down to their car. I offered them outside resources and tried a few other things, but unfortunately, their constant fighting ultimately ended in divorce.

Fighting steals joy. Depending on your life situation, you may have had to "fight" to survive at some point. I think about refugees fleeing war. I think about getting out of an abusive relationship. Maybe there was a season in your life when fighting was understandable as you tried to make it to a different level in life. Unfortunately, the challenge I repeatedly see in my office is where the "fight" to survive becomes part of the individual's daily temperament. Everything and everyone is a fight waiting to happen. A fighter can be identified by constantly fussing with their boss, arguing with family and contradicting the most innocent people in life, such as a store clerk or a child.

GIVING YOUR LIFE IN TOTAL SURRENDER TO GOD MAKES ALL THE DIFFERENCE.

The fighter's attitude is "I can do it myself," but a fighting life is a life void of joy. The solution to fighting is surrender. Giving your life in total surrender to God makes all the difference. That is where we find joy.

Ask yourself a few questions:

> Will this matter next year?
>
> Do I always have to be right or have the final say?
>
> Do I go from being mad at one person to mad at the next person?
>
> Is this a joy stealing pattern in my life? Is this the battle I want to pick right now?
>
> Have I thought about how I want to communicate, or am I just blowing off steam at someone else's expense?
>
> Do I want them to know how I feel, or should I take it to the Lord?

These questions will help you assess if you are in a posture of surrender or defense, and the difference can make or break the joy experienced in your life.

Let us take a sneak peak into Moses' leadership of the Israelites. Ultimately He surrendered to God, and by doing so, He brought joy to an entire nation of people.

"When the Israelites fled from the Egyptians, Moses led God's people straight into a situation that caused them to cry out, 'Was it because there were no graves in Egypt that you brought us to the desert to die? What have you done to us by bringing us out of Egypt? It would have been better for us to serve the Egyptians than to die in the desert!'" (Exodus 14:11-12)

With the Egyptians quickly approaching on one side and the drowning Red Sea on the other, the Israelites were doomed. In faith, Moses reassured God's people, "Do not be afraid. Stand firm, and you will see the deliverance the Lord will bring you today. The Egyptians you see today you will never see again. The Lord will fight for you; you need only to be still" (Exodus 14: 13-14).

What happened next has gone down in history as one of God's greatest miracles of all time.

Under God's instructions, "Moses stretched out his hand over the sea, and all that night, the Lord drove the sea back with a strong east wind and turned it into dry land. So the waters were divided, and the Israelites went through the sea on dry ground, with a wall of water on their right and left.

"The Egyptians pursued them, and all Pharaoh's horses and chariots and horsemen followed them into the sea. During the last watch of the night, the Lord looked down from the pillar of fire and cloud at the Egyptian army and threw it into confusion. He jammed the wheels of their chariots so that they had difficulty driving. And the Egyptians said, 'Let's get away from the Israelites! The Lord is fighting for them against Egypt'" (Exodus 14:21-25).

That day every single man in Pharaoh's army drowned in the Red Sea, and every single Israelite made it across the sea and onto dry land.

With His mighty hand, God fought the battle that only He could fight and win. Following that epic miracle, Moses led God's people in joyous praise. They sang to the Lord, giving Him all the glory. Because of Moses' great faith, their joy was complete.

> Dear God,
> I am helpless without your intervention. I cannot do this myself. I need you. Please come and fight for me. I surrender to your will and your ways now. In Jesus' name,
> Amen.

Surrendering to God's plan leads to a path of experiencing joy while fighting for our way pushes us off the joy path and into a pit of misery. Consider where you are holding too tightly to your own ways, and ask God to help you release your grip and surrender to Him. Then prepare yourself for a waterfall of joy.

REFLECT
choose one or two questions

Whether on your own or in a community of others, ask these questions and apply them to your life.

- What is your favorite carb?

- Tell us about a grade school fight you witnessed or participated in.

- Were you closer to your father's parents or your mother's parents? Describe your relationship with your grandparents.

- How does your family show affection first? Words, hugs, acts of service, quality time or giving gifts?

PRAY
this sentence prayer aloud as a group

Dear Lord,
I choose to trust you today.
I "want to want" you more.
I "long to long" for you.
Increase my desire.
Draw me with your Holy Spirit.
Amen

READ
take turns reading aloud

NUMBERS 11:1-2
Now the people complained about their hardships in the hearing of the Lord, and when he heard them, his anger was aroused. Then fire from the Lord burned among them and consumed some of the outskirts of the camp. When the people cried out to Moses, he prayed to the Lord, and the fire died down.

PSALM 34:1-4
I will bless the Lord at all times; His praise shall continually be in my mouth. My soul shall make its boast in the Lord; The humble shall hear of it and be glad. Oh, magnify the Lord with me, And let us exalt His name together. I sought the Lord, and He heard me And delivered me from all my fears.

2 CORINTHIANS 12:7-10
My grace is sufficient for you, for my power is made perfect in weakness. Therefore I will boast more gladly about my weaknesses so that Christ's power may rest on me. That is why, for Christ's sake, I delight in weaknesses, in insults, in hardships, in persecutions, in difficulties. For when I am weak, then I am strong.

EXODUS 14:13-14
Do not be afraid. Stand firm, and you will see the deliverance the Lord will bring you today. The Egyptians you see today you will never see again. The Lord will fight for you; you need only to be still.

CONNECTION
Answer these questions together

What "stealers" have you faced recently? Was your "joy stealer" a small one or a big one?
Small stealers might include - receiving a lousy email, road rage, procrastination on a project, fussy kids or running late
Big stealers might include - cancer, marriage difficulty, financial loss or grief

Share a time when you chose to keep joy instead of losing joy despite your situation. How did that work out for you?

Read Numbers 11:1-2. What hardships have you been complaining about to God? Share one complaint (joy destroyer) that you will give up. What words or attitudes could you choose to replace your grumbling?

Read Psalm 34:1-4. Share a time when you opened your mouth in praise, blessing or magnifying God. How did you feel?

Read 2 Corinthians 12:7-10. How can you delight in weaknesses, insults, hardships, persecutions, or difficulties?

KEEP JOY WITH WORDS	LOSE JOY WITH WORDS
WORDS OF THE BIBLE	WORDS OF DOUBTING
WORDS OF POSITIVITY	WORDS OF COMPLAINING
WORDS OF PRAISE TO GOD	WORDS OF CRITICIZING
WORDS OF CONFESSION	WORDS OF SECRECY

MEMORIZE

The Lord will fight for you; you need only to be still.

Exodus 14:14

PRAYER POINTS

Read Exodus 14:13-14. Where in your life do you need God to fight for you? Share with the group, and pray about these requests.

GROUP CHALLENGE

Hold one another accountable this week to stop complaining and keep the joy.

Keep track on paper of all your grumblings. Bring a jar or box to the group next week and put all your complaints inside it.

GROUP ACTIVITY

Place one person at a time in the center of your group. Verbally express words of blessing or encouragement over them. Share the good that you see in them. Speak over them positive words of love.

Go shopping together for new journals (haha, I know, any good excuse to shop!)

Serve a meal at a food kitchen and talk to the women there who need God's love.

Journal
AT HOME

Write a prayer to Jesus as your first love. Share honestly about any place in your life that has lost the joy of salvation. Ask Him to restore this love and happiness.

Make a list of lost people who need to know the Lord. Pray for them to "come home" to Jesus. Then pray for them individually by name.

BEAN AND CORN DIP
with a Southern Twist

INGREDIENTS

Salad

All cans should be drained and rinsed well. Depending on the size of your crowd you may use fewer or more cans. This does keep well in the refrigerator for several days.

1-2 cans of corn
1-2 cans of black beans
1 can of black-eyed peas
2-3 cans of Rotel tomatoes and green chiles
1 bunch of green onions
1 carton of reduced-fat Feta cheese
1 bunch of fresh cilantro

Dressing
1 cup of sugar
½ cup of apple cider vinegar
½ cup or canola oil

DIRECTIONS

I use scissors for my herbs and onions.
Rinse, drain and then pour the canned ingredients into a bowl.
Thinly chop the tops of a green onion.
Thinly chop the cilantro.
Break up the feta into small pieces and stir.

Meanwhile, boil and let the dressing cool, stir it well and pour over the dip. Let the dip cool in the refrigerator for several hours.

CHAPTER

Joy in Trials

Growing up in the South, we always had a pitcher of sweet tea and a container of pimento cheese in the refrigerator. There's nothing quite like sitting down in the cool of the house with a glass of brewed sweet tea when the temperature outside rises to 100 degrees or more. While I love sweet tea no matter the season, it is especially delicious and refreshing when the air is thick with humidity and the unforgiving sun scorches the landscape.

Joy in the Lord is like a tall glass of sweet tea. His joy is good no matter the circumstances, but His joy is all the sweeter when the surrounding circumstances are difficult and painful.

It may seem like an oxymoron, but suffering and joy can go hand in hand. I think of a beautiful rose. It is sweetly fragrant yet full of painful thorns. I remember feeling birth pains and holding my newborn within minutes of one another. It takes both sunshine and rain to grow a garden. I learned about joy in pain up close and personal on an assignment in Africa. I'll never forget this day because God opened my eyes to something unforgettable and mind-blowing. Go there with me now. You don't even have to endure the 24-hour travel across the ocean!

I was on a typical mission trip to Kenya when I met the "The Kakamega Girls" in a women's prison in Kakamega. Prior to arriving, I wondered what to expect and what level of suffering I would encounter. I asked myself, "Will I find joy at Kakamega? Can happiness be found amidst the pain?"

We pulled into a local grocery store with our mission team of six women, plus Bishop Evans and Mellen Achanga. The goal was to purchase much-needed items for the prison residents, items such as feminine pads, soap and a few plastic chairs. We filled our shopping carts to overflowing as fast as possible, even adding candy and an orange Kool-aid type juice. We worked together and anticipated what might bless the prisoners the most.

Meanwhile, a strange sensation came over me and the room began to spin. Leaning against store shelves, I thought, "Oh no, am I just nervous?" All of a sudden, I realized this was bigger than my nerves. Recognizing a supernatural attack, I acknowledged that a demonic resistance was trying to keep us from God's mission. This pressure was unlike anything I had experienced before. I muttered a quick prayer, "Help me right now, Lord Jesus!" Not wanting to alarm the entire group, I asked my dear friend Karen to walk with me for a minute because the room was still spinning. Together we walked down a long corridor to an unkempt restroom, and again, I felt a weird tingling and numbness come over me.

Still confused, I thought, "Hmm, maybe I ate something unusual." Once in the restroom stall, I boldly prayed aloud. A memorized "overcomers" prayer flowed out of my mouth, releasing the power of scripture.

> "My body is a temple of the Holy Spirit. Redeemed, cleansed and sanctified by the blood of Jesus. My members, the parts of my body, are instruments of righteousness yielded to God for His service and His glory. The devil has no place in me, no power over me and no unsettled claims against me. All has been settled by the blood of the lamb and by the word of my testimony, and I love not my life unto death. My body is for the Lord, and the Lord is for my body!"
>
> *(Corinthians 6:19, Ephesians 1:7, 1 John 1:7, Hebrews 13:12, Romans 6:13, Romans 8:33-34, Revelation 12:11, 1 Corinthians 6:13)*

The back of my neck bristled with the intensity of pushing back the darkness in the spiritual realm. Not wanting to alarm Karen, I pressed on in confidence. I finished praying and closed the stall door. Incredibly and instantly, I felt better. Thankful I did not worry the team, I quickly caught up with the group and returned to the van. As I regained my bearings and found my seat, I felt God as my rescuer sitting beside me. His presence was undeniable, and I knew that He was fighting an unseen battle for me, our team and the women in Kakamega. I was thrilled to be back on a mission!

Pulling through an opened gate onto a partially graveled and dirt driveway, we spotted an armed soldier guarding the main entry that was fenced in with barbed wire. A woman in charge came out to greet and usher us through several levels of security - first through two sets of barred doors and then to a security office where we had to make clearances. Her eyes smiled with kindness as she asked us to sit down for a series of security questions and instructions. Next, she asked us for our passports and to sign documents before entering. I recognized in my spirit that this woman needed encouragement, and I made a mental note to bless her with money before we left.

Once cleared, we entered through a third gate. Chickens ran across the dust-covered ground, not a blade of grass in sight. Matching black and grey striped laundry hung on a clothesline. Then we passed a cold concrete block building with grey barred windows peeking out of the top. I later learned that this was the high-security section for long term inmates, some even charged with murder or other serious offenses. I saw aluminum buildings surrounding the property painted a mix of bright chipped colors. These buildings housed women charged with lesser crimes. Approximately 100 women lived there in the dorm-style setting. Children under age three were allowed to stay with their mothers, and I saw several moms carrying babies on their hips. My heart flipped and flopped as I saw them 30 feet ahead of me, waiting patiently under the open-air canopy. I whispered under my breath,

"Father in heaven, meet us here and give us words of life and comfort for these precious women."

Because many of the prisoners knew the Lord, they invited friends to our meeting in hopes of introducing them to the joy of knowing Jesus. I was shocked to discover that the atmosphere where the women had gathered was positively electric! They had great anticipation for our visit and welcomed us with singing and dancing.

Most were barefoot and had short, shaved hair. There were no chairs available, and all were sitting in striped dresses on the bare ground. I was beginning to understand why we purchased a few plastic chairs to bring as gifts. We were told that they had very few material items, some even going without underwear.

Each member of our team shared a personal story of pain or disappointment. Giving testimonies of God's intervention in our lives united us and quenched our thirsty souls. We were deeply connected with them despite the color of our skin, language barrier or country of birth. Their mouths were smiling, and their hearts softened as they listened. Eyes were full as they began to see the hope available to them and sparkled as a belief for a new future became real. Remember Mary and John at the foot of the cross? At that moment, they were seen, noticed and loved by Jesus.

THESE WOMEN WERE ALSO SEEN,
NOTICED AND LOVED BY JESUS.

It was now my turn to give a message. I wanted them to learn about the gift of the cross, and so I shared about the power that forgiveness has over hurts and betrayals. This news was life to them, and as I spoke, they came alive with hope. Before our time ended, I decided to challenge them toward salvation. I asked, "Would you like to receive Jesus into your heart as Savior and leader?" Many hands went straight up in a big yes and then instantly back down. I thought,

"Oh no! In fear, all hands were back down." They were afraid, and our opportunity seemed lost. "God, only You can help us reach them," I prayed under my breath.

Saving the day, Bishop Evans Achanga stood up and spoke so smoothly in their language that even the babies listened. I sat down on a bench, praying for the Lord to help us while Evans talked. God nudged me, "Show them your passport." "Ok, Lord? I don't know why, but yes, I will." I heard this urgency again, "Show them." Before all was lost, I jumped back up and asked, "Would you like to see my passport?" They immediately reengaged and gathered around, fascinated to see it.

I shared with them that I would be unable to go back home if I lost my passport. Even though I was communicating through a translator, they clearly understood a touchable illustration. I told them that we all need a passport to enter heaven and having their names stamped in the Lamb's book of life is possible. What is this stamp? It is simply welcoming Jesus to live in your heart. "Do any of you want to get an all-access pass today? If so, come up front here, and we will pray with you." I held my breath, closed my eyes and waited for what seemed like an eternity. When I lifted my head and opened my eyes, five women and one baby stood right in front of me. They came forward with over-whelming courage. In front of their peers, they admitted their sins. These attentive women received forgiveness and confessed their love for God. Lives were saved, stamped and sealed forever. That was the day of salvation for many Kakamega girls! This could be your day too!

"For he says, 'In the time of my favor I heard you, and on the day of salvation I helped you.' I tell you, now is the time of God's favor, now is the day of salvation" (2 Corinthians 6:2).

We didn't leave them without first offering them our gifts. It seemed like a wedding with all the hugging, singing and dancing that broke out! God was tangibly near. He saw them, heard them, visited them at their house and gave out passports! Joy was there inside those prison walls.

Take Heart and Overcome

Joyous hope can coexist with hurt, but the world does not understand this. Instead, the world is steeped in self pleasures and chasing temporary fixes for despair. Worldliness searches but cannot find deep abiding joy. Even Jesus Himself wants us to overcome, and He reminds us to take heart in Him despite difficulties or grief. He offers us peace because He knows that life has many troubles.

"I have told you these things so that in me you may have peace. In this world, you will have trouble. But take heart, I have overcome the world" (John 16:33).

So what happens when life takes a wrong turn and we suffer? How can we hold on to joy in life? For starters, go ahead and feel it. Denying discomfort, sadness or ache only leaves room for procrastination in the healing process. Experiencing joy is not about squashing the hard or ignoring sadness but acknowledging it exists. Communicate back to Him everything weighing on you. Grieve, mourn and wail before Him. Take some time to give God your misery. Tell him. Baptism by fire is when you go through difficulty and cling to God instead of ignoring or denying Him.

"You turned my wailing into dancing; you removed my sackcloth and clothed me with joy" (Psalm 30:11).

Tears of Joy

I could hear tears in her voice when Amanda called me on the phone to say thank you for the new bedroom furniture. I wondered how crushed she must have felt after investing twenty-five years into a marriage that eventually fell apart. The gift of furniture from our family was just one way God had found to soothe her aching soul.

A few nights earlier, Doyle and I pulled into the driveway still pumped with energy about a student worship night with our church ministry. "Honey, I want to give Amanda our second bedroom suite." Silence in the car. "Ok, Jenn, we can do that, but why?" "I found out that she has nothing to sleep on right now."

Out of dozens of volunteers, Amanda in particular was a favorite with the students because she connected so well with young people. Her ability to relate and care for them was top-notch. They knew she was authentic. Her recent separation from her husband was news to us. Upon further investigation, I learned it was an abusive situation. She had fled from the home and was staying in a one-room apartment nearby.

Doyle lifted the entire bedroom suite, new mattress and box springs into a borrowed truck, and we arranged with a friend to get the keys to Amanda's apartment. Though we were a young family with two toddlers, it was our pleasure to load up the furniture and deliver it to her apartment. We also purchased a lavender and white linen set complete with shams and a dust ruffle to compliment the bedroom set.

While Amanda was at work, we set up the entire room. I was upset to see that she slept with a pool raft on the floor of an empty apartment. We made the bed, hung curtains and even put flowers on the nightstand. She came home a few hours later to this heartwarming gift, and you can imagine the look on her face. I love that she continued working and serving God despite her difficulties. He positively was her answer. Like iced sweet tea on a hot day in the middle of a Tennessee summer, He provided just what her thirsty soul needed.

Tears of Sorrow

Tears really are therapeutic, aren't they? Somehow our tears allow us to release the emotions that are bottled up inside. Similarly, scripture tells us that God bottles our tears, and He records each one in His book.

"You keep track of all my sorrows. You have collected all my tears in your bottle. You have recorded each one in your book" (Psalm 56:8).

Tears of joy or sadness are valuable to God, and He saves them in a bottle. God cares and values our tears when we share them with Him. They show God that we trust Him. In His grace, He comforts us and trades our tears for His abundant joy.

"Those who sow with tears will reap with songs of joy. Those who go out weeping, carrying seed to sow, will return with songs of joy, carrying sheaves with them" (Psalm 126:5-6).

What a gift we have in God that He counts and keeps our tears, comforts us in our pain and returns to us His neverending joy. When is the last time you wept in the presence of the Lord? Run to Him with your tears, and let Him sit with you in your pain. I trust that He will provide for you as He did Amanda and the "Kakamega Girls," filling you with His joy in exchange for your sorrow.

The Hard Questions of Life

Call me weird, but I love the book of Job because he exemplifies a principle about the questions we all want to ask. Whenever we don't understand the anguish we feel, our temptation is to doubt that God is good. When we begin to question the very goodness of God, it leads us down a slippery slope of depression.

Job was a great communicator with God. He told Him everything. Though Job asked God questions, he didn't question Him about His excellent nature. There is a difference. Job had complete confidence in the qualities and character of God. If we want to come through the difficult places in life, we can bring our questions to God in an honorable way of respect and wait for the answers knowing that some questions will never be answered this side of heaven.

While Job also turned to his friends, they were not helpful to Job in their attempts to support him. One of the best things you can say to a friend when she is suffering is, "That is horrible; I'm so sorry." When someone is in a hard place, it is not for us to go in and shine things up with our "joy-remarks." Rather, let the Holy Spirit do the heavy lifting. Sit with your suffering friend, and remember that God's promises are faithful and true. His Spirit will do the work. He will prove himself.

HE WILL PROVE HIMSELF

We don't want to "whitewash the fence" for ourselves or others. Imagine painting a fence white, but instead of painting the whole fence, you only paint the front of the fence. From the road, the fence looks cheery, clean and crisp, but from the back, the fence appears worn and ugly. Emotionally we are guilty of this. When we attempt to ease another's pain with flippant remarks such as, "at least it wasn't worse," or "I'm sure God has a better plan," or "everything happens for a reason," we whitewash the fence around the sorrow and pain.

Instead, simply sit with the ones you love in their painful place. Sometimes the best way to support a friend is to simply be with them. Being with is so much better than almost anything you can say, and as you sit in the hard place, you can commit to praying when your friend doesn't have the words and commit to faith when your friend's faith is weak.

Over the years, I have sat with and prayed with several mothers who had babies in the NICU. These moms came in distress, and their tiny babies needed a miracle. These are the moments when it is better for me to just simply be with them, holding their hands, validating their tears and remaining strong in faith on their behalf.

"Let their flesh be renewed like a child's; let them be restored as in the days of their youth'—then that person can pray to God and find favor with him, they will see God's face and shout for joy; he will restore them to full well-being" (Job 33:25-26).

"That God would be willing to crush me, to let loose his hand and cut off my life! Then I would still have this consolation—my joy in unrelenting pain—that I had not denied the words of the Holy One" (Job 6:9-10).

> Dear God,
> I humble myself before You because I have many questions.
> These are my questions _____.
> Can you help me to understand? I'm in a difficult place, but I'm looking to You for answers. I choose to put my trust in You as my comforter, healer, deliverer and provider. I know You are good, and I know that You love me. In Jesus' name,
> Amen.

Come Closer to the Fire

"Therefore, since we are receiving a kingdom that cannot be shaken, let us be thankful, and so worship God acceptably with reverence and awe, for our 'God is a consuming fire'" (Hebrews 12:28-29).

I still remember when my teenage son came home from sixth-grade camp. He was on fire for Jesus having drawn closer to God during nightly worship around the campfire. Having attended many youth camps myself, I could imagine what he experienced and felt, sitting with a group of like-minded kids, singing, praying and sharing testimonies. Something about the firelight piercing the darkness after a long day of camp activities seems to soften us and open our ears to what God has been trying to teach us throughout the week away from home.

It reminds me of Paul and Silas. While not around a campfire, Paul and Silas experienced a campfire-like experience after a long time away from home on mission for God. Rather than camp, they were in a prison, and it was there that God softened their hearts and opened their ears to a miracle.

Paul and Silas were no strangers to difficulty. They ministered together and were grateful to have one another. Their story goes from wonderful baptisms and salvation to dark and dramatic when arrested in Acts chapter 16. What a horrific intrusion to the planned mission.

Can you imagine the embarrassment and fear they felt in that hour? Paul and Silas were flogged naked for the sake of Christ. Yes, it was a nightmare. I don't like to think about how bad it must have been. Onward to prison, they sat together under the eagle eye of guards. I think I would have been crying, screaming or something crazy, but not Paul and Silas. They chose a different path. Like kids around a campfire, they decided to praise the Lord.

WHILE PRAYING AND SINGING
HYMNS, SOMETHING MYSTERIOUS
BEGAN TO HAPPEN

The Lord sent an earthquake to set them free. God has a way of moving the mountains in our lives when there is no logical explanation in sight. He can and He does, and He will move them for you. The jailer freed Paul and Silas, and then the jailer brought them to his home and introduced them to his family. His entire household was baptized that day.

This jailer witnessed Paul and Silas, in all their wounds, reach out to God. I love the jailer because he eventually fed them and bandaged their sores. He chose not to harm himself and instead turned in the right direction. The biggest question you and I have to answer is this: are we willing to be like Paul and Silas? Are we willing to choose to worship and pray even in our suffering? Or perhaps, are we willing to be like the jailer? He shared this God event with his entire family, ultimately impacting their lives for eternity.

Is it a Test, Trial or Temptation?

As believers in Christ, we all need to stay aware, on guard and ready. Recognizing our situation is half the battle, so we must ask ourselves a few questions. Is this a test that God has allowed in my life? Can I identify this as an extended trial? Or am I experiencing a temptation? Which one is it, and how should I respond to God during these events?

All three of these can steal our joy if we allow them. Let's look at each - tests, trials and temptations, and learn how to maintain our joy in each situation.

TESTS

TESTS ARE A DIFFICULTY THAT GOD HAS EITHER ALLOWED OR PROMPTED IN YOUR LIFE.

"Dear friends, do not be surprised at the fiery ordeal that has come on you to test you, as though something strange were happening to you. But rejoice in as much as you participate in the sufferings of Christ, so that you may be overjoyed when his glory is revealed" (1 Peter 4:12-13).

My wedding ring is gold with diamonds. Two of the diamonds are baguette diamonds from Doyle's mother, and another diamond is from his great grandmother. I don't know the exact monetary value of the ring, though I imagine it's one of the most costly items that I own. I do know that the ring's sentimental value to me is priceless.

Similarly, God sees our lives as both valuable and sentimental because we matter so much to Him. He chooses to test and refine us because of His great love for us. He wants our character to be pure as gold. One test is how you respond when someone treats you poorly or says something hurtful. Other tests are related to material things such as giving and financial stewardship. He also tests us relationally. Are we willing to forgive? These are just a few examples of tests.

God brings tests to examine our hearts and draw us closer to Him. We don't generally enjoy tests. God values us and cares about the lessons He wants to show us. He wants us to pass and I don't want to retake it! As a teacher, God wants you to learn to trust Him. God is a good parent. He is more interested in the development of our character than the situation at hand.

GOD IS
A GOOD
PARENT.

On a Sunday morning, the zoo visited our church for the kid's ministry. A couple animals that arrived were a lazy sloth and an armored armadillo. The sloth could barely keep his eyes open! The sloth reminds us that we can't be lazy during tests or we will fall asleep and miss the mark. On the other hand, the armadillo had a problem because he would hide in his shell and roll to the corner of the room. In that corner, no one could play with him or see his fascinating qualities.

Tests are an opportunity for us to be honest with God and give Him our problems. Choosing to recoil and hide from God or people during a test doesn't work.

During a test, the Holy Spirit might prompt you to repent or change your way of thinking to line up with His. God might say to you, "Why are you embarrassed? Was it your fault? If so, have you asked me for forgiveness?" Sometimes it is not our fault, and we are carrying shame. Other times we need to repent. Regardless, God wants your heart on Him. If we are carrying guilt or shame, God is there with us, helping us to respond in forgiveness, grace, mercy and love. If we have sin that we need to repent, God is there with us, offering forgiveness, grace, mercy and love. You are a loved child of God, and He is always with you.

"Instead of your shame, you will receive a double portion, and instead of disgrace, you will rejoice in your inheritance. And so you will inherit a double portion in your land, and everlasting joy will be yours" (Isaiah 61:7).

"The apostles left the Sanhedrin, rejoicing because they had been counted worthy of suffering disgrace for the Name" (Acts 5:41).

During a test:
- Choose joy over shame, embarrassment or disgrace.
- Ask yourself, are you willing to be identified with Christ?
- Allow the test to draw you near to God.

TRIALS

TRIALS ARE LONG. IN A TRIAL, YOU EXPERIENCE SOMETHING PAINFUL OVER THE COURSE OF TIME.

"...sorrowful, yet always rejoicing; poor, yet making many rich; having nothing, and yet possessing everything" (2 Corinthians 6:10).

"Consider it pure joy, my brothers and sisters, whenever you face trials of many kinds" (James 1:2).

Trials take time and build character. Lengthy issues teach us to listen, wait, pray and endure, not alone but with God. Problems are where we develop the fruits of the Spirit, such as long-suffering, patience, and yes, even joy. Trials are so long that we learn to humble ourselves and become teachable. During these droughts, we learn, we grow and we do hard things. Our focus becomes more on heaven and less on earth.

A young couple had their house on the market for nine months and still no sale. In this time, they learned to pray together and balance their budget. During the waiting, they realized they were emotionally attached to "stuff." Eventually the house sold, and they were ready for their move with altered priorities and a new perspective.

One day I talked to my friend Grace, and she shared with me how she would eat bread with sugar or mustard on top as a young girl because her mom struggled financially to keep the refrigerator full. As a grown-up, she was talking to her mom one day, and her mom said, "I stayed home with you kids for ten years but didn't have any money to take you anywhere or do anything." Grace replied, "Mom, I didn't miss that part. I remember you reading us the Boxcar Children and Little House on the Prairie series from the library, playing with dolls, and on a special day making homemade strawberry fruit roll-ups." This encouraged her mom to see she had loved her kids and they remembered the love, not the material lack that resulted from the trials that she endured.

Finding joy in lack or in dry times can be difficult, but it is possible. Famine comes in different ways. Famines can come in more ways than food. You might experience a famine of finances, friends or dreams. I'm not sure what you are in the middle of right now but ask God for wisdom and a strategy to help you through.

- Famine is hard. Famine without God is harder.
- Trials are long. Trials without God are longer.

"Though the fig tree does not bud and there are no grapes on the vines, though the olive crop fails and the fields produce no food, though there are no sheep in the pen and no cattle in the stalls, yet I will rejoice in the Lord, I will be joyful in God my Savior. The Sovereign Lord is my strength; he makes my feet like the feet of a deer. He enables me to tread on the heights" (Habakkuk 3:17-19).

"In the midst of a very severe trial, their overflowing joy and their extreme poverty welled up in rich generosity" (2 Corinthians 8:2).

TEMPTATIONS

TEMPTATIONS DRAW YOU AWAY FROM GOD.

"No temptation has overtaken you except what is common to mankind. And God is faithful; he will not let you be tempted beyond what you can bear. But when you are tempted, he will also provide a way out so that you can endure it" (1 Corinthians 10:13).

The difference between a test and a temptation is simple. Tests draw you near to God, and temptations pull you away from God. In a God-allowed test, you should be asking Him for help instead of expecting Him to change the circumstance.

SOMETIMES IN HIS GRACE, HE DOES
ADJUST THE SITUATION BUT USUALLY NOT
UNTIL WE RELY ON HIM FOR ANSWERS.

Temptations may seem harmless at first but generally consist of something either unhealthy or ungodly for us if we so choose to participate. We usually don't need whatever it is that is tempting us. Furthermore, temptation snowballs into additional sins such as greed, dishonesty or breaking any of the ten commandments.

Temptations can come at us in small or large ways. Doyle and I were eating a breakfast sandwich at Hardee's with my in-laws when suddenly we heard a deafening, high-pitched noise and then a crash. We jumped up from the table and headed toward the exit door. A teen driver had driven his car through the wall and windows into the fast-food restaurant. Thankfully, no one was hurt. The atmosphere was tense as the concerned employees called 9-1-1 and took care of the situation. We got out of their way and drove home.

This may seem simple, but we had a choice to make. Would we change our plans for the rest of the day? Would we let fear and nervousness ruin our time together? When you are visibly shaken, it is tempting to worry or shut down in panic. Instead, we chose peace. We prayed for all involved, and then we kept our plans and enjoyed our day together. God wants to help us out of even the smallest temptations, and He will if we cry out to Him. Victory over temptation brings joy. When we stop and ask, the Holy Spirit will come into a situation and bring us comfort. That's His job.

"When anxiety was great within me, your consolation brought me joy" (Psalm 94:19)

The Joy of the Lord
IS WITH YOU IN YOUR PAIN

What God continues to teach me is that His joy never fails. Through female prisoners in Kenya, through my hurting friend Amanda, through the tears, the questions, the prison and the fire, God keeps teaching me that where He is, there is joy. His joy is not an eraser of pain or a mask to our sorrows. It's not a magic potion that turns back time or plunges us past the hard and into the future. His joy finds us in our hurting, broken and pain, and it brings warmth, hope and promise.

When we seek Him in our trials, choose Him in the test and turn to Him during temptation, we give way for His joy to seep in, strengthening us as we take another step forward. It's not always a rushing rainbow or sudden smile, but it is just enough, sometimes only a morsel, to lift and carry us to the next moment. And by His grace, it never runs out no matter how dark our world becomes.

"You became imitators of us and the Lord, for you welcomed the message in the midst of severe suffering with the joy given by the Holy Spirit"(1 Thessalonians 1:6).

Discussion Guide

REFLECT
choose one or two questions

Whether on your own or in a community of others, ask these questions and apply them to your life.

- Where is your hometown? What was your favorite food or drink from there?

- What is the longest flight you have taken, and where did you go?

- What zoo animal do you relate to the most? Sloth, armadillo, lion, giraffe, monkey or other?

PRAY
this prayer aloud as a group

Dear God,
I humbly come before You. I have many questions because I'm in a difficult place, but I'm looking to You for answers. I choose to put my trust in You as my comforter, healer, deliverer and provider. I know You are good, and I know that You love me. In Jesus' name,
Amen.

QUICK REFERENCE

JOB 6:9-10 "That God would be willing to crush me, to let loose his hand and cut off my life! Then I would still have this consolation—my joy in unrelenting pain—that I had not denied the words of the Holy One."

1 PETER 4:12-13 "Dear friends, do not be surprised at the fiery ordeal that has come on you to test you, as though something strange were happening to you. But rejoice in as much as you participate in the sufferings of Christ, so that you may be overjoyed when his glory is revealed."

2 CORINTHIANS 8:2 "In the midst of a very severe trial, their overflowing joy and their extreme poverty welled up in rich generosity."

ISAIAH 51:3 "The Lord will surely comfort Zion and will look with compassion on all her ruins; he will make her deserts like Eden, her wastelands like the garden of the Lord. Joy and gladness will be found in her, thanksgiving, and the sound of singing."

JAMES 1:2 "Consider it pure joy, my brothers and sisters, whenever you face trials of many kinds."

PSALM 56:8 "You keep track of all my sorrows. You have collected all my tears in your bottle. You have recorded each one in your book."

ACTS 16:25-26 "About midnight Paul and Silas were praying and singing hymns to God, and the other prisoners were listening to them. Suddenly there was such a violent earthquake that the foundations of the prison were shaken. At once all the prison doors flew open, and everyone's chains came loose."

CONNECTION
Answer these questions together

Read Job 6:9-10. Share a time in your life when you went through a difficult place yet like Job, held tight to your faith in God. What joys did you experience in the midst of the suffering?

Remember the story of Amanda and how God provided a bedroom suite for her? How has God provided for you during a troubling time?

Read Acts 16:25-26. Paul and Silas had a worshipful campfire experience. Have you ever had a camp renewal in your life? In light of what happened in vs 25 how do you think Paul and Silas felt?

Have you ever been falsely accused, severely beaten or jailed? In those circumstances how would you still trust God's plan for your life? How did worship and prayer make the difference for Paul and Silas? In what way will it change your current situation?

What did you notice about the jailer, how can you relate to him?

Read 1 Peter 4:12-13 and 2 Corinthians 8:2. Can you identify if you are in the middle of one of the following: test, trial or temptation? Which one? Share your plans to overcome with joy. Has God shown you anything or spoken to you through this season? If so, what?

MEMORIZE

Those who sow with tears will reap with songs of joy.

Psalm 126:5

PRAYER POINTS

If you are in a temptation, share it honestly with the group and pray to be free.

If you are suffering under a long trial or learning lessons through a difficult test, pray for one another to have godly character and to be strong with endurance.

GROUP CHALLENGE

Set a bottle in your kitchen window this week to remind yourself that God holds your tears.

Reach out to someone who is in a long trial and call, visit, or take them meal.

GROUP ACTIVITY

Plan a campfire with s'mores, songs and testimonies.

Journal
AT HOME

Identify if you are experiencing a test, trial or temptation.

Write out the lessons you are learning and the character you are forming.

Pray for the strength to endure your trial, and write about the miracles and joys you have witnessed along the way.

Write a prayer for help asking God for a way of escape from any temptations. Make a determination in your behavior to say no to the enemy and yes to God's ways.

Journal your questions to God.

INGREDIENTS

Cake

1 large instant vanilla pudding
1 Container of Cool Whip
1 Box of Graham crackers
3 cups of milk

Chocolate Topping

¼ cup of milk
1 cup of sugar
¼ stick butter
1/3 cup cocoa
1/8 Tsp salt
1 Tsp Vanilla

DIRECTIONS

Cake:

Mix pudding and milk well.
Fold in cool whip.
Butter a 9x13 pan.
Put a layer of crackers in pan.
Spread half of pudding on crackers.
Add a second layer of crackers.
Spread the remaining pudding on crackers.
Top with crackers again.

Chocolate Topping:

Combine milk, sugar, cocoa and salt.
Boil for one minute.
Remove from heat.
Add butter and vanilla, stir in.
Cool and spread on top layer of crackers.

Store in refrigerator and enjoy!

This recipe is from my dear friend Rachel Wojo.

CHAPTER

Joy in Victory

Like it or not, all of us live on this roller coaster called LIFE. We are here on this earth breathing, living and walking around all the while the earth is slowly rotating on its axis. The question we each have to answer is how then shall we live? Do you want to live upset, worried or depressed? Or do you want to walk out your days in love, peace, hope and ahhh yes- JOY!

So what is the strategy to live a celebrated life of joy? It doesn't mean that we are jumping, loud or exuberant every moment. It means that we are satisfied, we are comforted, we are seeking God and we are listening to Him.

As followers of Jesus, we have an all-access pass to a lifetime of joy. Because He already won the battle, we can live in victory both here on earth and for eternity in heaven. So what does it look like to live a life of victory? How do we live joy in victory, and what does that even mean?

Gideon's Victory and Joy

Gideon was a prophet, judge and military leader of God's people during a time when the Israelites were turning to worldly gods rather than the Lord. As a result, God gave them, His people, into the hands of the Midianites who were ungodly in their ways.

"Gideon was threshing wheat in the winepress, out of sight of the Midianites. The angel of God appeared to him and said, 'God is with you, O mighty warrior!' Gideon replied, 'With me, my master? If God is with us, why has all this happened to us? Where are all the miracle-wonders our parents and grandparents told us about, telling us, 'Didn't God deliver us from Egypt?' The fact is, God has nothing to do with us— he has turned us over to Midian.' But God faced him directly: 'Go in this strength that is yours. Save Israel from Midian. Haven't I just sent you?' Gideon said to him, 'Me, my master? How and with what could I ever save Israel? Look at me. My clan's the weakest in Manasseh and I'm the runt of the litter.' God said to him, 'I'll be with you. Believe me, you'll defeat Midian as one man'" (Judges 6:12-16).

Gideon didn't think he had much to offer God or the people of Israel who were dishonoring God and being defeated by their enemies. God said to Gideon time again that He would be with him and help him to be a strong warrior. Despite Gideon's insecurity, he listened to God. In time, he grew as a valiant and victorious leader and ultimately won the battle and defeated the Midianites with only three hundred men.

Gideon gives us a picture of a life lived in victory and a life of joy as a result of living in that victory. What I love about the picture we receive from Gideon's life is his victory was a process, not a one-time exchange. In other words, he was faithful to God one step at a time, and one step at a time, he walked toward victory and joy.

Here's the victory process that we witness in the life of Gideon.

- Have a conversation with God, sharing your fears and concerns.
- Be still and listen for His guidance.
- Lean into God's response to you. Receive and stand on the promises of His word.
- Start taking steps to follow Him in courage.
- Praise and enjoy God along the way.

What if you used that process as an overlay on your life? Where in the victory process are you? Where do you need to begin? Are you ready to start living in joy and victory?

JOY COMES IN THE MORNING.

"For his anger lasts only a moment, but his favor lasts a lifetime; weeping may stay for the night, but rejoicing comes in the morning" (Psalm 30:5).

Crickets squeaking, frogs bellowing, woodpeckers pecking and birds chirping as the sun rises in the mountains over Lake Norris. I am reminded of Jesus when He rode into Jerusalem to the praises of the people. The Pharisees, wanting the people to stop praising Jesus, challenged Him publicly in an attempt to quiet the crowd. Jesus responded that even if the people stop praising, the rocks will still shout praise to Him. I thought about that passage as I listened to the symphony of bugs, bees and birds in the woods, "If I don't wake up and praise Jesus, even the insects will cry out. All creation knows to sing His praise."

As the steam rose off my "on lake time" coffee mug, the sun and my heart rose in praise, full of joy. Just as the sunrise is unfailing, I am reminded that I can depend on God. His presence, His mercy and His joy greet me each morning without fail, just like the sunrise.

Thirty years prior, Doyle and I spent our first full day of marriage in the Tennessee mountains. Now, three decades later, we were celebrating what God has done and the goodness He has shown us through all these years. These are the times of exuberant delight to proclaim His majesty. I never want to lose the principle of pausing to acknowledge the triumphs. Reminiscing about God's faithfulness brings joy to keep like a feather in a cap.

Where can you look back and see the hand of God? It's never too late to pause and say, "Today I celebrate the goodness of God in the land of the living." Allow the freshness of a new day to renew your attitude and the grace of the morning to set your mind on treasured things. This pause deserves a joy-filled prayer to recognize that God has been faithful and good.

Dear God,

You are welcome in my heart. I love You. I praise you. You are trustworthy. I see the works of Your hand, and I rejoice. I reminisce over your faithful goodness. Thank you for loving me.

Amen

"Satisfy us in the morning with your unfailing love, that we may sing for joy and be glad all our days" (Psalm 90:14).

"I remain confident of this: I will see the goodness of the Lord in the land of the living" (Psalm 27:13).

Find a reason to dance

"Then young women will dance and be glad, young men and old as well. I will turn their mourning into gladness; I will give them comfort and joy instead of sorrow" (Jeremiah 31:13).

When was the last time you stopped everything simply to praise God for His goodness in your life? Consider this question: What is your ultimate win with God right now? Your win will look different than mine. Maybe God's goodness is shining brightly through physical healing, a new baby, freedom from addiction, a new job, salvation or even clear direction about your future. Whatever it is, have you paused to thank Him for the victory?

God's people have a set pattern of stopping their daily grind to honor and recognize God's tried and true qualities. Scripture is full of celebrations that acknowledge what God has done, and some of those celebrations are still honored today in both Christian and Jewish traditions (for instance Easter, Passover, Hanukkah and Christmas). Each year at our church, we set aside time to praise God and give awards to our devoted volunteers. At this annual celebration, we eat together, and then we share testimonies of answered prayers. Sometimes we even dance until late at night. Are you willing to take time with your Christian friends or family and simply have a festive occasion for no reason except to recognize God's goodness in the land of the living?

"It was not by their sword that they won the land, nor did their arm bring them victory; it was your right hand, your arm, and the light of your face, for you loved them" (Psalm 44:3).

"For you, Lord, have delivered me from death, my eyes from tears, my feet from stumbling, that I may walk before the Lord in the land of the living" (Psalm 116:8-10).

Joy Comes
FROM FOLLOWING THE HOLY SPIRIT

In Chapter One, we discussed joy as a fruit of the spirit. We focused on joy as a fruit that needs to be grown, developed and cultivated. However, joy and fruit are only byproducts of the most critical component of the phrase "fruit of the spirit."

The vital part of that phrase is the spirit. What Spirit? The Holy Spirit. In Chapter Three, I shared about the trinity including the Holy Spirit who is our guide, nudging us and pointing our hearts toward God's presence and plan. The Spirit brings freedom to our lives by giving us discernment about our choices, decisions and steps. The Bible describes the Holy Spirit like a dove. He can freely come close to you as you listen and welcome Him. He can also fly away at any hint of ungodliness.

I jumped off the bus in sixth grade, thrilled to be home so I could play and not think about school for a few hours, when I heard an audible voice say two words to me, "Look up!" I paused on the sidewalk a few feet from the front door and looked up into the sky to see a white dove flying over the roof of our house. "Mom, mom, mom! Guess what I just saw? This beautiful white bird was flying over the house!" Mom was sitting in the living room at the piano. She just happened to be writing a song. The bird was a confirmation of all God had been teaching us about the Holy Spirit. I can hear the keys and her voice as she played the song for me.

Sweep over my soul Holy Spirit, sweep over my soul heavenly dove, sweep over my soul Holy Spirit and make me a channel of love.
A channel prepared for the Master. Creator, Savior, and friend.
Sweep over my soul Holy Spirit and make me a channel again.

The Holy Spirit is the key to victory in our lives. When we live in step with the Spirit, we experience more of what God wants for us, ultimately leading us to joy. When we are out of step with the Spirit, we miss out on the wonder and awe that God has for us, including joy.

I challenge you to begin connecting more deeply with the Holy Spirit, asking him to stay near and lead you to a life of victory and joy.

> God,
> I pray that you would help me to be sensitive and aware of the Holy Spirit. I want the fruit of the Spirit - joy! I want more and more of your Holy Spirit in my life. Show me anything I need to stop saying or doing. I want to please You.
>
> Amen.

"And I will pray the Father, and He will give you another Helper, that He may abide with you forever— But the Helper, the Holy Spirit, whom the Father will send in My name, He will teach you all things, and bring to your remembrance all things that I said to you" (John 14:16,26 NKJV).

Clear Victory

Steve Kabachia called one afternoon inviting Doyle to Kenya to lead a training conference for pastors. Excited about the opportunity, Doyle brought the news to me and said, "Jennifer, the church will pay my way on this mission, and I think we can personally afford to pay for one of us to go along with me." I stopped in my tracks, my heart skipping a beat because this was an opportunity of a lifetime. I also stopped because I just could not comprehend going without my two sons. "They must go with us," I said to Doyle, "We can't leave the boys behind.

I want them to experience this as well." He said, "Of course, I do too, but it is financially impossible to take all four of us. Choose one of the boys, or choose yourself, but I need to buy the tickets soon. You have no later than three weeks to decide."

I pondered this dilemma for a couple of days, prayed about it, and then I returned to Doyle with an idea. "Honey, what if I sell the house so all of us can go together?" He replied, "Sell the house?!" In my absolute determination to take our entire family to Kenya, I was ready to sell it all to experience God's goodness with my brothers and sisters in Africa.

I WAS READY TO SELL IT ALL TO EXPERIENCE GOD'S GOODNESS WITH MY BROTHERS AND SISTERS IN AFRICA.

Either because he thought there would be no way that our house would sell or because he just wanted to squash me from further outlandish ideas, Doyle responded, "Ok, you can try to sell the house. We don't have a lot of time to make this decision, and I doubt it will sell within the time frame needed to recoup the money and buy airfare, but if selling the house is what you want to do, then give it a shot."

I quickly placed a *For Sale By Owner* sign at the end of the driveway, and then I got to work preparing our home for a sale. I tidied, cleaned, steamed and painted. The house was as ready as it would ever be. Not only was it a long shot to try and sell our home in such a short amount of time, the timing really could not have been worse. It was 2012, and the housing market was slow. It was a buyer's market, and our home was just one of the hundreds of other homes that families had to choose from.

I didn't let that stop my stubborn will and determination. I began fasting and praying, asking God to allow this trip for all four of us, even at such a huge sacrifice. I truly loved my home, yet something profound inside of me was pulling me toward missions. It must be the Holy Spirit. Surely if God wants us to go, He will make a way possible. The longest three weeks of no-showings were nearing an end, and there was not one phone call about our house. I sat on our back porch depressed and talking to God. "My understanding was that You would want all four of us to go. Can't You make a way? I thought my yielding to You by selling the house would be pleasing to You, Lord. I felt a deep tug to go to Kenya, and I believe that tug is from You. Can't we go?" I heard the Lord say clearly, "Are you sure you want to go? This could mean the beginning of a new mission for life." I slowed a minute and responded, "Yes, I am sure." I didn't realize at the time that I was walking in faith.

The day before the tickets had to be purchased, I felt emotionally defeated. There were still no bites on the house. All I had to show for the last three weeks were many, many long chats with the Lord. I was still fasting, restless and prayerful, and so I decided to drive to church to work in my office alone. Once I arrived, I kept praying, "Ok, Lord, it must be the right mission but wrong timing for our family. Who do you want to go with Doyle? I will accept your choice for us. Amen."

As soon as I said "Amen," the phone rang, and it was a lady I knew from the community. She said, "Jennifer, I have inherited some money from my mother, and I would like to purchase your home with cash." I couldn't believe my ears. Literally out of thin air, this near acquaintance called me up and offered to buy our home - a cash offer! ONLY GOD! We were going to Kenya! My husband, our two boys and I could afford to go! God answered my prayer in the nick of time, and I'm so glad He did!

"Then Job replied to the Lord: 'I know that you can do all things; no purpose of yours can be thwarted'" (Job 42:1-2).

I certainly am not suggesting that you sell your house in order to buy a couple of expensive plane tickets. What I am suggesting to you is that our God has no limits when it comes to His victory plan and the joy that follows in our lives. By staying open to His possibilities, we discover opportunities that we never dreamed before. As a result, we take part in His abundant joy, a fresh reservoir that never runs dry.

The experience of unexpectedly selling our house to a woman who fell into a large sum of money and then taking the money from that sale to buy tickets to follow God on mission to Africa, changed our lives. By following God and His Spirit, we found victory and joy on the other side. Some of the highlights of that experience are truths that serve as reminders to my soul, even today:

- The path to victory mountain is through the valley of uncertainty.
- The hard work of trusting God is staying open.
- For strength to rise, slow down and reflect.
- Your greatest strengths are invisible.
- Steps of faith lead to miracles that start with the unexpected.

"Until now you have not asked for anything in my name. Ask and you will receive, and your joy will be complete" (John 16:24).

"Bring joy to your servant, Lord, for I put my trust in you" (Psalm 86:4).

The Big Five

God's passionate love is on display at Masai Mara, one of the most outstanding animal reserves and safari sites in the world. Quite literally, the vast migration of the wildebeest animals passing from Tanzania across the river in Kenya is called the eighth wonder. This safari was a reward for my sons after two weeks of ministering to pastors in church meetings and conferences in the busy city of Nairobi. The safari lands, spread out for miles and miles, are like a piece of heavenly rest provided by God. Masai tribe warriors wearing bright red plaid tunics welcomed us with a steaming bowl of roasted carrot soup, rice and potatoes that tasted like a dream.

After a solid night's sleep outdoors in a tent, we laughed as exotic monkeys greeted us from the treetops with four-feet long swinging tails of black and white fur hanging down like a rope. Six am awakened us to the reality that we were not on a bear hunt but a quest to see the "Big Five," as they say in Kenya. The big five are the great lion, leopard, rhino, elephant and African buffalo. Kenyans are proud of these God-given creatures, and rightly so. Though the giraffes don't make the top five, they are number one, and I could not wait to see them in their natural home setting.

We were also there to see the rare, once-a-year migration of wildebeests. Our jeep was packed with Doyle, our two boys, Steven Kabachia Jr. and a picnic lunch. Set with sunscreen, a camera and anticipation, we began along the highly bumpy road, and soon we witnessed dozens of zebras in all their glory mingling with wildebeest and the occasional funny warthog. I was reminded of the Lion King movie as we sang, "Hakuna Matata, what a wonderful day" in Swahili (which means no worries). It was a good day.

Hundreds and hundreds of these black moose-like creatures dotted the landscape. Our driver found the exact spot where they would cross the river one by one and turned off the Land Rover engine so we could watch. The wildebeests formed the most unbelievable single file black line that stretched for miles, as far as the eye can see. I marveled as the wildebeests must have listened to God's still small voice to bravely cross the river filled with alligators and hippos ready to snap their jaws for a bite. I'll never forget the sight as long as I live. It is just as described in National Geographic. The Great Migration is considered one of the world's most extensive wildlife spectacles on earth.

Victory as a Team:
YOU, GOD AND HIS PEOPLE
ARE A WINNING COMBINATION

A journal entry I wrote after the African safari to see the Big Five:

> *Even animals celebrate victories and mourn defeats together as a team. We watched in wonder while a family of lions snacked on their Wildebeest capture for lunch. We discovered an enormous black rhino hiding in the brush and four spotted leopards prowling in confidence and gliding in front of our vehicle without a care in the world. Perhaps the most fascinating of all was observing an empathetic elephant family as they clung together mourning one of their own. Actual tears wet their leathery cheeks. I learned that they would stay together for a week in the same spot to mourn their loss before piling sticks and logs to make a memorial for their loved one. I was awestruck.*

As for this mama bear (me), my heart was whole because our family victory was together in Africa. All the way from Columbus, Ohio, our precious family of four sold our home and traveled twenty-four hours to minister to pastors, their wives and kids in Kenya. We were honoring God together, and He allowed us the special treat to witness the wildebeest migration and Kenya's "Big Five." I sat and stared in awe of the realization that God is in every detail of creation and all aspects of our lives. Seeking His will and plans for our lives is worth the effort. We should never be ashamed to lift our hands in thanksgiving and to revere His holiness and majesty.

We finish our animal quest with a picnic under the canopy of blue sky while my favored giraffes roam nearby. I count ten. I think it is their eyelashes that I love the most. I wonder what beauty serum they recommend to get such luscious length?

GOD REVEALS HIS NATURE TO US IN NATURE.

Now I understand why the Kenyans are proud of these safari lands and God-given creatures.

God reveals His nature to us in nature. Humanity has no excuse but to look to God, and many Kenyans do just that in total love and commitment to Him as an example to us. As enthralled as I was with the animals on safari, those moments did not hold a candle to how I felt the day of the mattresses.

Joy in Victory

At the end of my trip to Kenya, the one in which we visited the women's prison, our final joyous celebration was giving mattresses to widows at the women's conference. These widows had lost their husbands to disease, war or poverty, and their lives were at risk as well. Without a husband's protection, many of the women had endured sexual or physical abuse, or both.

Our visionary leader, Mellen Achanga, led a team of women throughout the surrounding villages. They went house to house with a clipboard to make notations of each situation. Looking for widows and orphans, they first invited them to our conference, knowing full well that many would have to walk several miles to attend. Second, the leaders noted any physical needs in their homes, such as medicine, food or a bed. Of course, their top priority was to offer the women and children the hope of Jesus. They gave each woman a biblical team name and badge such as Esther, Deborah, Mary or Ruth. This was a practical way to keep track of them and make follow-up easier later on.

In response to the list of needs, our church purchased 450 mattresses plus twenty vinyl-covered mattresses for invalids. On the final day of our meeting, additional widows and many orphans arrived. Their heads were covered to keep their hair clean and neat. I was impressed with their sweet smiles and warm attitudes of gratitude.

Off to the side was a mountain of brightly-colored mattresses rolled in a bundle. The vibrant colors and patterns gave my spirit a jolt of joy. As it was the end of the conference, spirits were high, and we celebrated with the women and children, praising God for His goodness and salvation.

That day's celebration was like nothing I have ever experienced in my lifetime. The widows danced, cried out in joy and bowed in gratitude. Raising their hands in the air, they lifted their strong voices in thanksgiving to God. The space was filled with exuberant energy, wide smiles and the glory of the Lord.

One by one, we called out the names of the teams: "Esther," and then, "Deborah," "Mary," and then "Ruth." When their name was called, the team stepped up. Greeting each woman individually, we handed out mattresses to every woman in attendance. After the last team received their mattresses, Mellen offered an encouraging message in Swahili. Though I could not understand her words, I understood the response that erupted from the women when Mellen was finished. It was pure joy.

Without missing a beat, the women returned to singing, dancing and praise. Now with their mattresses lifted above their heads, they continued dancing under the bold sun, a team of sisters and children together in victory and joy.

"May we shout for joy over your victory and lift up our banners in the name of our God. May the Lord grant all your requests" (Psalm 20:5).

"But may the righteous be glad and rejoice before God; may they be happy and joyful" (Psalm 68:3).

An Umbrella of Joy

Joy. The entire world population seeks to find it, but only one person can deliver true, everlasting joy. Joy, by worldly quests, is elusive. The search for it only leads to a greater and deeper search. There is not one thing on this earth that can offer long lasting, sustaining joy, but there is someone, and His name is Jesus.

True joy can be found and attained, but in order to receive it, we must surrender. Rather than finding joy through more money, power, fame, fortune, stuff, friends or social media likes, we must release control of our lives and let God direct our path. Through salvation in Jesus, we can find, know and live with joy, no matter the dumpster fire that burns around us. In fact, we not only can know true, everlasting joy in Jesus, but we can also live victoriously in it and spread it freely wherever we go.

In victory, we live under an umbrella of joy, shielding us from chronic despair and hopelessness. Joy isn't an eraser or mask to our pain. Joy is a gift that honors our pain and brings light into the darkness, guiding us forward one step at a time.

I hope and pray that this book has helped you discover greater joy in your life. I trust that the Holy Spirit is working in you even now as you reflect on the journey of understanding, searching and finding the joy of Jesus throughout your life. I pray that you become a joy spreader, gifting His joy to everyone you meet. I know that His joy will meet you in your valleys and wave mightily in your mountaintop moments.

It has been pure joy to travel this journey with you. As I've climbed through a very personal health battle, His joy has been my strength. Thank you for joining with me. I have no doubt that God has used this book, this journey and this quest for joy to support my healing and give me hope.

His victory is forever, and His joy is yours to keep.

The joy of the Lord is your strength.

REFLECT
choose one or two questions

Whether on your own or in a community of others, ask these questions and apply them to your life.

- What awards or recognitions have you received? What did you do to earn them?

- How do you like to celebrate birthdays, holidays or anniversaries?

- Describe a memorable victory celebration you attended.

PRAY
this sentence prayer aloud as a group

Dear Jesus,
You are my victory. Teach me to walk in Your ways of joy, peace and hope for my future. I welcome Your Holy Spirit to show me your plans and instructions as I move forward. I choose joy and to celebrate You in my life. Thank you for everything.

Amen

# READ

JUDGES 6:12-16

Gideon was threshing wheat in the winepress, out of sight of the Midianites. The angel of God appeared to him and said, "God is with you, O mighty warrior!" Gideon replied, "With me, my master? If God is with us, why has all this happened to us? Where are all the miracle-wonders our parents and grandparents told us about, telling us, 'Didn't God deliver us from Egypt?' The fact is, God has nothing to do with us—he has turned us over to Midian." But God faced him directly: "Go in this strength that is yours. Save Israel from Midian. Haven't I just sent you?" Gideon said to him, "Me, my master? How and with what could I ever save Israel? Look at me. My clan's the weakest in Manasseh and I'm the runt of the litter." God said to him, "I'll be with you. Believe me, you'll defeat Midian as one man."

1 TIMOTHY 5:3,5

Give proper recognition to those widows who are really in need. The widow who is really in need and left all alone puts her hope in God and continues night and day to pray and to ask God for help.

PHILIPPIANS 4:8

Finally, brothers and sisters, whatever is true, whatever is noble, whatever is right, whatever is pure, whatever is lovely, whatever is admirable—if anything is excellent or praiseworthy—think about such things.

CONNECTION

Answer these questions together

READ JUDGES 6:12-16

- How did God encourage Gideon that he had what was needed to fight and win against the Midianites?

- Like Gideon, describe a time in your life when you felt not good enough for the task at hand.

- How has God given you courage to win against discouragement or the battles you have faced?

- What did God say to you?

- Was it audible, through a friend or His word?

Jennifer describes the experience of the church mission team helping widows in Kenya.

- Who have you helped?

- How did that make you feel?

- Where do you feel God is challenging you to serve Him?

- How might obeying God bring joy to your life?

READ PHILIPPIANS 4:8

- Share something from the list in this scripture that you would like to "think upon" this week.

- How might this verse give you a fresh perspective?

- Share a recent victory. How did you celebrate?

PRAYER POINTS

Pray that God will help you to mature in Him and connect more deeply with the Holy Spirit in order to live a life of joy.

Pray for any widows or orphans you know personally or around the world.

Pray over any upcoming celebrations, and pray that your family and friends would experience the love and salvation of God.

GROUP CHALLENGE

Have you thought about dancing together?

IDEA: play worship music (live or pre-recorded) and dance, clap, bow and sing to the Lord in joyful thanksgiving.

Meet with widows, single moms or orphans, one on one as mentors or in a group.

GROUP ACTIVITY

Find orphans or widows in your city and show them the love of Jesus in a practical way, or go on a mission trip together.

Plan a victory party and celebrate what God has done through this journey of joy.

Journal
AT HOME

Pour out your heart to the Lord about a mission local or afar where you feel He is drawing your attention.

Perhaps God is calling you by His Holy Spirit to pray more and more. Make a list of what He wants you to pray about and journal the scriptures God gives you to confirm this calling.

Spend time reflecting on the victories in your life, and make plans for your next celebration. Be intentional.

INGREDIENTS

Fruit
3 C fruit
1 C sugar (to taste)
Topping
1 1/2 C flour
1 Tbs. oil
1 Tbs. sugar

DIRECTIONS

1. Pour water over fruit and sugar and simmer on stove in pan.

2. Pour into pan to bake.

3. Mix topping ingredients together. Add milk until the batter thins.

4. String dough over fruit.

5. Sprinkle sugar over it.

6. Bake at 375 degrees until browned.

KAKAMEGA, KENYA

JENNIFER WITH BISHOP
ACHANGA AT KAKAMEGA

WOMEN PRAYING AT CONFERENCE

JENNIFER
WITH
MELLEN
ACHANGA

BISHOP STEVE AND JENNIFER KABACHIA

JENNIFER AND
DOYLE WITH
BISHOP EVANS
AND MELLEN
ACHANGA

MASAI MARA:
LION

MASAI MARA:
WILDEBEEST
MIGRATION

MASAI MARA:
SAFARI ZEBRAS

JENNIFER WITH JENNIFER KABACHIA AT LOITOKITOK

GIVING MATTRESSES TO WIDOWS: ANGEL,
JENNIFER, SHERI, COURTNEY, KELLIE AND KAREN

FOR SMALL GROUPS

These are suggestions on how to get the most out of the group experience. Consider meeting for eight weeks with the last week a dinner celebration.

Take these STEPS for a wonderful group experience:

COMMUNICATION

Communicate by sending an email, text or call ahead of time to each member and cover steps 1-3. Give them the time, schedule and location of your group (in your home, at church or on zoom). Encourage them to bring a friend.

GROUP SIZE

This JOY study is good even if you have a small group of two or three friends. However, if you go beyond sixteen gals, gather to fellowship and then separate into two groups of eight and reconvene at the end for fellowship again.

GET THE BOOK

Encourage your group to get a book copy of *Simply Joy* or the pdf version. If there is a financial burden, please contact Jennifer Jackson for a complimentary copy for that person. Prepare yourself ahead of time for the group as much as you can.

READ

Have your women read one chapter per week before they attend the group. Discussion questions are at the end of each chapter for convenience. Encourage them to write in their books as a journal. You will lead from the discussion guide at the end of each chapter.

CREATE A SAFE PLACE

Remind the women that your group is a safe place. What is said here stays here. Complete confidentiality is a must for comfort. This is not a counseling or advice group. Be patient with your group. It is ok to give them some time to answer. If they are stuck, be willing to share openly from your life as a leader. Make sure you allow them plenty of time to share as well.

APPLICATION

This is a Biblical Application group. The desire is for women to seek God, look into His word and apply it to their daily lives. An in-depth study can happen individually at home. Your group should be a place for women to gather, no matter their spiritual maturity level. Hopefully, you will have some brand new believers who always add life and excitement and some seasoned ones who add wisdom and experience to the conversation.

HOMEWORK

Prompt the women to thoroughly **read the scripture references** at the end of their chapter before the group. Many will not do this, and that is ok. If you want to feel more prepared, read the scripture references in advance. The desire is to keep this simple yet rich. Go as deep as you enjoy.

ICE BREAKERS

Choose one or two ice breakers. When a group is brand new, you might need more to get them talking. Once a group is comfortable, you will use fewer questions. If the icebreaker goes too fast, then you might have time for three questions. This should be a light and welcoming time for anyone to participate.

SCRIPTURE

Say the memory verse together aloud in unison, and then the short prayer that incorporates the verse. This gives everyone a chance to participate as well. These are at the back of each chapter.

Have your apprentice leader or someone in the group choose and read aloud one of the scripture passages.

CONNECTION QUESTIONS

Use this section in whole or part. It depends on your group, time frames, size and personality of the group. Some will only get through a couple of questions, and others will finish everything. Do what works best for you and enjoy!

PRAYER & PRAISE

End with the prayer and praises. Use the prayer point section as it applies to your unique group. Prayer is something you want to make sure to save time to include. Teach them to pray aloud and for one another. You might even meet an extra time just for prayer.

FELLOWSHIP TEA OR DINNER

Share the load, ask someone in your group to host the fellowship tea or dinner.

FEEDBACK

Feedback would be appreciated for the next study. Please email jennifer@jennifer-jackson.org with tips or suggestions for future studies. Thank you for serving the Lord, and may these eight weeks be a JOY in your life ~ Jennifer

The people of Kenya
HOLD A PIECE OF MY HEART

No place on earth has taught me more about living with abundant joy. My Kenyan brothers and sisters are deeply generous and hospitable, willing to give their last morsel to both the neighbors and strangers in their lives. I remain committed to the widows and orphans who are especially vulnerable in the parts of the country that already suffer so much.

If you want to make a difference in the life of an orphan or widow in Kenya, go to www.jennifer-jackson.org and search for Kenya under the Outreach tab.

There are two options:
1) **Simply Go**, and join us on our next mission trip and women's conference.
2) **Simply Give**, and help an orphan or widow for one month or even a year.

WWW.JENNIFER-JACKSON.ORG